# Text Me

# Text Me

## Ancient Jewish Wisdom Meets Contemporary Technology

*Jewish Resources for Understanding, Enbracing, and Challenging Our Evolving Digital Identities*

Jeffrey Schein
*with Brian Amkraut*

HAMILTON BOOKS
*Lanham • Boulder • New York • London*

Published by Hamilton Books
An imprint of The Rowman & Littlefield Publishing Group, Inc.
4501 Forbes Blvd., Ste. 200, Lanham, MD 20706
www.rowman.com

6 Tinworth Street, London SE11 5AL, United Kingdom

British Library Cataloguing in Publication Information Available

**Library of Congress Cataloging-in-Publication Data Available**

ISBN 9780761871781 (pbk. : alk. paper)
ISBN 9780761871798 (electronic)

♾™ The paper used in this publication meets the minimum requirements of American National Standard for Information Sciences—Permanence of Paper for Printed Library Materials, ANSI/NISO Z39.48-1992.

To my wife Deborah whose journeys of mind and heart have often been parallel and sometimes wonderfully overlapping with my own. She has been a partner in thought as well as life.

And to my children (Ben, Jonah, and Hana) and their spouses (Robyn, Rachel, and Greg) who have been so often kind and gentle with my foibles both digital and human.

And to the holy one blessed be she who each day renews the act of creation and grants me the optimism and equanimity to endeavor to live creatively and ethically in the digital age.

# Contents

# PART III: JEWISH LEARNING AND LIVING

# PART IV: COMING FULL CIRCLE

# Acknowledgments

I have been blessed with the careful editing of Rabbi Reena Spicehandler and Jean Lettofsky and the accurate proof reading of Beth Friedman Rommel. Rabbi Elliot Dorff also did a useful edit of the volume.

The following communities and institutions have played an instrumental role in supporting this volume.

The Covenant foundation provided the initial funding for the project of the same name as this book.

The Jewish Education Center of Cleveland (particularly Family Educators network members Judith Schiller, Jill Cahn, Gloria Grischkan, Iree Reich, Amy Pincus, Barbara Rosenfeld, Beth Mann, Rabbi Estelle Mills, and Marla Wolf) were partners in generating the pedagogic templates that became the core of this volume.

The "cousins club", a small group of millenials including Rachel Zukrow, Ilene Kosoff, Jonah Schein, and Ari Greenberg who provided meaningful feedback at the earliest stages of the book and project.

The synagogue community of the Twin Cities and a number of Reconstructing Judaism congregations across North America were the sites that allowed the project take on the challenges of adult learning.

The Mordecai M Kaplan Center for Jewish Peoplehood and the Laura and Alvin Siegal Institute for Life Long Learning provided important thought partners for the project.

I am particularly grateful for the critical collegiality of my friend Dr. Brian Amkraut, author of a chapter in the book and commentator. I am also appreciative of my havruta/study partners Sherwood Malamud and Earl Schwartz who studied a selection from Talmud and from the work of Emanuel Levinas with me.

I am deeply appreciative of the enriching insights of the commentators to this volume: Reverend Terri Elton, Dr. Mary Hess, Imam Sami Aziz, Rabbi Elliot Dorff, Rabbi David Teutsch, Rabbi Mira Wasserman, Rabbi Marc Margolius, Dr. Brian Amkraut, Rabbi Nathan Kamesar and Rabbi Hayim Herring, Peter Eckstein, Dr. Adina Newberg, Rabbi Steve Sager, Rabbi Michael Cohen, and Amelia Gavurin.

*Part I*

# THE BIG PICTURE

## Chapter One

# Why This Volume?

A double entendre is an *ambiguity of meaning arising from language that lends itself to more than one interpretation (Merriam Webster)*. The agony and ecstasy of my teaching life as a rabbi, educator, academic, and spiritual coach these past six years is wrapped up in the double entendre in the title of this volume, *Text Me: Ancient Jewish Wisdom Meets Contemporary Technology*. The term "text" can mean a source of wisdom in Judaism (as in studying sacred Jewish wisdom). It can also mean a form of contemporary communication (as in "texting" someone).

There are overlaps, synergies, conflicts, dissonances, and creative tensions to be discovered between these two uses of the word text. This volume explores the interplay of these meanings in multiple directions, but with a single purpose in mind. That purpose is to help readers understand their own rich and complex relationship to technology from Jewish, spiritual, and ethical perspectives.

Any book about technology runs the extraordinary risk of becoming dated between the time of conception and execution. To cite just one example, in 2012 when I first began the workshops that led to this book there was a great deal of concern among parents about the digital footprints of their teenagers. The conventional wisdom was that any comments or pictures posted on social media stayed with their child into adulthood. Just think of the difficulty of explaining away an indelible remark or image to a college admissions officer of a prestigious school! By the end of that year, however, the new technology of Snapchat offered a different reality, one of posts that disappeared in time sensitive ways. Though imperfect, the new technology allayed many parental fears.

The speed of technological change and adaptation also affects my personal positioning in relationship to technology. Many a life-long friend finds it odd that I am writing this volume. At best I am in the middle of the pack in regards to keeping up with technological change. I always begin my workshops by joking with participants that if they came for advice about purchasing a PC or an Apple or finding a new, innovative digital technology, they must have misread the notice about the workshop. In general, I have tried to compensate for my own status as a digital immigrant by working closely throughout the project and book with an advisory board of millenials and professors of educational technology. There are also web-based extensions of the book where new developments can be named, tracked, and analyzed, thus keeping the volume fresh and relevant.

In the end, however, I do not claim to be an innovative thinker about technology per se. Rather, my hope is that the volume offers the reader the three gifts of PERSPECTIVE, BALANCE, and SELF-AWARENESS in their relationships with technology. These capacities will arguably serve the reader well in any changed technological landscape. At the beginning of each chapter I have placed a reminder of the balance of these three gifts that I hope the reader will glean from the chapter. The gift I believe most significantly operative in the chapter is capitalized and bolded; the other two appear in lowercase letters.

I have found that the best way I can make these gifts accessible to readers is to give myself permission to speak in a very personal voice throughout the volume, peppering the social, scientific and academic with personal vignettes. I agree with Parker Palmer that we do our most authentic teaching when we teach ourselves (Palmer, 1998, 24) Though I appreciate why some readers will want to pigeonhole the volume into the categories of formal or informal, academic or personal, I have tried to resist these labels. The label I would choose is one that reflects my intention of making the volume *dialogic* and *conversational.*

Even when the reader and author are not in immediate physical proximity to one another, I imagine a conversation that might begin in the reader's mind and be given later virtual reality on the Text Me website designed for ongoing conversations mentioned later in this introduction. To encourage this process I have placed a blank "Dear Evolving Self" page at the end of each chapter along with a scroll symbol. The reader is invited to pause before moving on to the next chapter and reflect upon new insights by journaling on this page. The reader can also change the salutation to "Dear Jeffrey" or "Dear Commentator" and affirm, extend, or challenge points that have been made.

In the course of my teaching I have come to understand that while each of the three gifts has value for all, there is also a developmental/generational dimension that distributes value unevenly across the life-cycle. For people my age (Boomers and beyond) I believe it is PERSPECTIVE that is most appreciated in understanding one's relationship to technology. We have, after all, lived through multiple technological revolutions. For Millennials, who are often "sandwiched" between generations BALANCE seems to be the great gift. For Generation Z, who have many shifts in their relationship to technology still ahead of them, SELF-AWARENESS might be the greatest gift.

The value of these three gifts may not be immediately obvious or appreciated by all readers of any generation. The restart Life center of Seattle suggests (https://netaddictionrecovery.com/hat) technology is a taboo topic linked to "persuasive design," a phenomenon of intentionally harnessing psychological constructs to make technology all the more enticing, even addictive. In fact there is a sense in which discussing technology takes us into dangerous psychological territory. The psychoanalyst Rollo May argued that every age has a characteristic taboo, a subject that cannot comfortably be discussed. The nineteenth century Victorian taboo against discussing sex in public had been replaced by a twentieth century taboo about discussing death and dying by the time May wrote *Love and Will* in 1969. (May, 1969, 105). That taboo too has passed. We discuss both topics now with relative ease. In the twenty-first century we have a new cultural taboo. It is called technology. As with all taboos, we are barely aware that we are not having conversations about this important aspect of our lives.

It sounds counter-intuitive. Technology is so pervasive that we can hardly imagine our lives without it. Yet we treat technology and its role in our lives in functional rather than religious or dialogic ways. In our minds, it is a means to an end of enhanced communication capacity and increasingly, a tool for resculpting our own identities. From a Jewish perspective, rarely does it receive the kind of appreciative nod that the Jewish value of *hakarat hatov/ appreciation of the good* would suggest when technological ingenuity scaffolds our comfort, effectiveness, or core ethical humaneness. We are more likely to curse our technological instruments when they don't work, than praise them when they do. Still less does technology receive the reflective attention Einstein demanded for all science, when he claimed that human beings have developed a plethora of scientific and technological means and a paucity of worthy ends toward which we might deploy those means.

Famously, Marshall McLuhan once observed "first we shape our tools and then our tools shape us" (McLuhan, 1967, 24) My conviction is that we desperately need a round three where we talk back to the ways we have been shaped by our tools. This, however, can only happen through dialogue. I hope this volume will "break the silence" about the fierce complexity of technology's role in our lives through an amplified Jewish voice. (COM)

## THE HOW OF THE BOOK:
## THE TOOLS OF JEWISH TEXTUAL TRADITION

The following tools of the Jewish textual tradition are utilized extensively throughout *TextMe: Ancient Jewish Wisdom Meets Contemporary Technology*:

**Midrash**/Rabbinic commentaries designed to expand upon the meaning of a given Jewish text;

*Pardes*/Adventures in Jewish Complexity—Pardes is an acronym that points to the complexity of our processes of understanding the world. Any single phenomenon has dimensions of *peshat* (transparent meaning), *remez* (hints of a mystical reality), *derash* (moral concern), and *sod* (ultimate grounding for our place in the world). The initial letters of these four strategies form the acronym.

*Hashkafot*/The worldviews of Jewish thinkers, with an emphasis on the relationship to the world of tools and technology suggested in that worldview;

*Sugyot*/Focused conceptual, religious, and ethical issues explored in the Talmud;

*Responsa*/Rabbinic legal rulings beginning in the 9th century C.E. that raise questions about how we should act in situations either unanticipated or ambiguously described in earlier Jewish law;

**Musar**/Conscious attempts to strengthen our ethical and spiritual virtues through self-awareness and introspection;

*Machlokot*/Divisions of opinion that lead to sacred, respectful argument;

*Teyku*/An acknowledgement that certain debates are not easily reconcilable and have no one single answer; we thus invite Elijah, the prophet who, according to Jewish tradition will announce the coming of the messianic age, to have the last say.

To use a digital metaphor, these tools are our spiritual algorithms. They are time-tested ways of understanding the purpose of Jewish and human life in the face of a world whose pace of acceleration is dizzying. They serve as filters of an ethical and spiritual sort. One can make a reasonable case for government and industry to externally regulate aspects of our digital lives, but ultimately it is the self-regulation of individuals and communities utilizing their most deeply held Jewish and human values that can most effectively respond to the potentials and challenges of new technologies. In 2019—when the political right can define its relationship to media by railing at "fake news," and the political left can bewail the impulsive and compulsive twittering of our President—a personal, introspective, moral compass of *our own* relationship to technology arguably is of even greater value. (COM)

## THE WHO OF THE BOOK: MULTIPLE AUDIENCES

In the following chapters I explore these traditions in greater depth, as well as provide concrete suggestions for incorporating the insights gained into patterns of Jewish, ethical, and religious life. Though primarily aimed at the thoughtful adult Jewish learner and seeker, many activities are applicable to Jewish schools and congregations and other religious faiths as well. Those who consider themselves "spiritual but not religious" or simply appreciate Jewish wisdom as a subset of human wisdom might also find the volume of interest. For all readerships, I hope that this volume will serve as both a theoretical and practical guidebook, sparking insights generated by the collision of ancient wisdom and contemporary technological advances. An appendix at the end of the volume address the specialized learning needs of the different audiences.

There are two unique features of the volume:

As befitting any twenty-first century book, there are links to the *Text Me: Ancient Jewish Wisdom Meets Contemporary Technology* website where issues raised in the book can be further explored and also accessed in formats ready for teaching, learning, and self-exploration. When a particular selection in the volume is available as a ready to use teaching-learning tool, it is marked *TMW* for the Text Me website (www.textmejudaism.com)

One of the goals of the volume is to generate ongoing dialogue. In Jewish tradition there is no better vehicle for that purpose than *parshanut*/commentary. Since I consider both Torah and the ongoing process of interpreting Torah as encompassing all human wisdom, I have invited a wide range of commentators—Jewish and non-Jewish—to respond to passages in the book.

These include Reverend Terri Elton, Dr. Mary Hess, and Imam Sami Aziz, who were invited to deepen and enrich comments in the volume with insights from Christian and Islamic traditions. Jewish commentators include Rabbi Elliot Dorff, Rabbi David Teutsch, Rabbi Mira Wasserman, Rabbi Marc Margolius, Dr. Brian Amkraut, Rabbi Nathan Kamesar, and Rabbi Hayim Herring. Peter Eckstein and Etan Dov Weiss provide educational perspectives.

Dr. Adina Newberg and Rabbi Steve Sager offer perspectives gleaned from modern and contemporary Hebrew Literature. Rabbi Michael Cohen provides the perspective of a Jewish environmentalist. Amelia Gavurin, an organizer for Twin Cities Jew Folk, offers a millenial/Generation Z perspective. *COM* in the text guides the reader to the commentary sections of the volume where these expanded insights can be found.

## CONTENT OF THE VOLUME

The volume alternates between a focus on the impact of technology on individuals as global digital citizens (Jews and people of other faiths as well) and on the Jewish people as a collective entity. The first section of the book addresses the individual. The second section tells the larger story of technology in relationship to the Jewish people as a whole. In section three I attempt to weave together the individual and the communal stories into various dimensions of contemporary Jewish living and learning. Finally, in section four I propose a recursive journey back to the beginning of the volume, inviting readers to review key aspects of the volume and, to paraphrase T.S. Eliot, see some sections of the volume anew as if they were reading them for the very first time.

## COMMENTARY

*From Rabbi Nathan Kamesar*: I'm reminded here of the debate around action to mitigate, and hopefully ultimately reverse, the effects of climate change. Some argue that we must all do what we can to influence our own carbon footprints—limiting our use of electricity, eating vegetarian diets, and the like. Others argue that this focus on individual responsibility unhelpfully shifts emphasis away from the more effective means of combating climate change that involve collective action, such as carbon taxes, a cap and trade system, or other policies that would ensure a comprehensive approach. While I agree that being conscientious, thoughtful, and even holy in our use of technology is imperative, there is no substitute for a national conversation around technology policy (and anti-trust implications, for instance) that will have great bearing on how technology impacts our lives.

*From Rabbi Mira Wasserman*: Missing here is the experience of Generation X, the cohort that comes in between the Boomers and the Millennials.

I came of age in the 1980s, before the digital revolution, but when the rise of video games was already re-configuring how people spent their time and built relationships. A new technological landscape shaped people my age, and contributed to an identity defined by *Slackers* and *Reality Bites* (two films that capture the spirit of the age).

Perhaps thinking generationally is no longer as helpful as it once was. The accelerated pace of change with regard to technology raises questions about what constitutes a generation. My youngest child is eight years younger than my oldest, and their formative experiences with technology—in school, at home, and in connecting with peers—are qualitatively different.

*From Dr. Terri Elton*: With the pace of technological changes accelerating, it has become easy to focus solely on the particulars of technology while ignoring other facets. An important aspect of the work educators and scholars bring to society is stepping back and reflecting on the impact these tools have on our lives and society. The work of this volume recognizes our time as a critical moment for reflection, not only for those navigating changes today, but setting the course for the future. This book does that not only from one person's perspective but gleaning from a diverse set of perspectives.

*From Rabbi Hayim Herring (commenting on persuasive design)*:
My reaction to the Mall of America's newest hook to lure people to shop for Christmas.

*Ellie the Elf Wants You on the Shelf*

*Make your pilgrimage to the high Temple of Shopping,*
*The one that surpasses them all (THE MALL).*
*In this frozen state, where spring comes late,*
*You pay to pray you'll find the right offering*
*in over 500 stores of cheap and chic housed together,*
*Conveniently over-shopping in any weather.*

*The Temple is large,*
*a faux Town Square.*
*Climate controlled, you breathe fresh recirculated air.*
*Meaningless street names lead you to nowhere,*
*because your destination is not a relation,*
*But a transaction without friction.*
*So, go on - treat people like they're fiction.*

*Instead find your help,*
*Ask the new holograph elf,*
*But beware -*
*You'll soon be inventory on tomorrow's shelf.*

© December 16, 2018 *Hayim Herring*
*(Based on the Mall of America introducing a holographic elf for Christmas*
*shopping; https://www.engadget.com/amp/2018/12/11/mall-of-america-hologram*
*-concierge/)*

Dear Evolving Self (Dear Jeffrey, Dear Commentator),

## Chapter Two

# First Master Text, *Siyag*/Fence

**PERSPECTIVE**, self-awareness, balance

The first text is about "fences" in Jewish Law and life. In the Talmud, a *siyag*/ fence is understood as a form of protection from committing a transgression. We distance ourselves from a possible infraction by imposing a a *chumrah*/ stricter stringency beyond the letter of the law on our behavior. Thus one could, according to one Talmudic opinion, fulfill the commandment not to mix milk and meat by changing the table cloth and beginning the milk part of our meal separately. However, Jewish Law generally imposes a standard of at least a three hour separation between eating a meat and milk product. Similarly, one could keep the Sabbath free of monetary commerce by not exchanging money. It should not matter if coins jingle in one's pocket. Yet, the "fence" around financial commerce extends the boundary to not touching money at any point during the Sabbath.(COM)

Of course fences have been enshrined in our Western consciousness as well by the famous 1914 Robert Frost poem "The Mending Wall". There Frost captures some of the paradox of the value of fences in our lives as he simultaneously suggests "good fences make good neighbors" and then argues with himself that before building the wall he wants to know exactly what is behind the fence he has constructed. As a metaphor for the digital age, we might ponder whether it is even possible or advisable to filter or fence off the multiple messages that come our way each day. Sealing ourselves off from the vital, unfolding online life of a culture can make us parochial and insular. Living without a protective digital fence screening us off from the intensity and immensity of communication is arguably equally dangerous.

Returning to our Jewish perspective, while the tradition of a *chumrah*/ stringency beyond the letter of the law is often thought to be a tool of the strict observers, there is another function of a fence more aligned with the purposes of this volume. A surprising insight can be found in *Sefer Ha-Aggadah/ The Book of Legends* (Bialik and Ravnitsky, 1992, 464). Rather than being simply a literal restrictive tool mechanically applied to every behavioral situation, a fence can be seen as serving an entirely different function, that of bestowing perspective, as suggested in the following midrash:

> Enter not into the path of the wicked . . . Avoid it, pass not by it; turn from it and pass on (Prov: 14–15). Rabbi Ashi said: The verse may be illustrated by the parable of a man who guards an orchard. If he guards it from without, the entire orchard is protected; but if he guards it from within, only the part in front of him is protected, while the part behind him is not protected.

Awash as we are in digital technologies, we post-moderns desperately need all the fences (understood as perspective bestowing boundaries) we can find as we try to understand the many ways that technology has reshaped our human and Jewish identities. It is useful here to suggest a connection between two phenomena: the flourishing of musar and other techniques of reflective centering and the overwhelming pace of technological change. We need to learn the art of "steadying ourselves" as we adjust to the numbing pace of technological change. (*TMW, COM*)

What happens when we momentarily step outside the all pervasive digital environment in which we live to view it, as it were, from beyond the fence? Seeing our digital selves from outside the fence of our regular rhythms of living can be disconcerting, even shocking. In the trailer to her film *Connected*, Tiffany Shlain shares the following personal epiphany: She had traveled across the country to visit a dear high school friend whom she had not seen in years. During their lunch together she is seized by panic. She had not checked her messages in six hours which makes her feel painfully disconnected. So intense is the discomfort and ensuing internal panic that she fakes having to go to the bathroom to check her messages. She ends the vignette by declaring "Oh, my God, what have we become" (Shlain, 2012, trailer film *Connected)*

The search for perspective triggered by this volume might in theory lead to "Oh my God" moments in multiple directions, suggesting both more and less use of technology. The volume will also be doing its work of helping the reader find balance in her relationship to technology if the reader says the same "Oh, my God" but with a different ending! "Time to get with it... I have fallen too far behind my own children and grandchildren in terms of my digital skills". Certainly there are other scenarios that fall between these two extremes of doing a great deal less or a great deal more with our digital lives. The goal in all cases is to increase self-awareness and agency. Readers who engage with the ideas in this book enjoy the possibility of reshaping their own relationship to technology.

We conclude our examination of this gift of personal perspective by inviting readers to see themselves in the big picture of their relationship to technology. Below are five composite stances gleaned from a survey of over three hundred Cleveland Jewish adults in 2012.[1] The meaning of the results is best understood through the lens of David Schon's and Chris Argyris's work on reflection (Agyris and Schon, 1996). Few of us wake up in the morning and say "Time to refresh and refine my thinking about technology." We rarely generate new theories about technology.[2]

Yet we each have "a theory in use" that guides our thinking and actions on a daily basis. By providing the individuals who took the survey an opportunity to step back and examine previously unexamined assumptions about their relationship to technology, we sought to create a link between the intuitions that guided them and the values they espoused. One can understand this book as having the same purpose on a larger scale.

The parents surveyed fell into the following five stances, which are more than purely descriptive as they involve at least a modest claim to normative prescription—what one should do in relationship to technology.

Stance 1: Adaptive Digital Navigator
It is quite *chutzpadik* (a cross between having audacious nerve and great arrogance) to think we are in control of this process: our only real choice is to flow with these powerful technological currents.

*Representative Survey Response:*
*Technology is central to my business and my clients' businesses. I couldn't serve them without it.*

Stance 2: Early Adopter
It is always valuable to be at the front of the user cycle. The earlier one jumps on board the more likely the person is to glean the long term benefits of every new piece of technology.

*Representative Survey Response:*
*It's more than a toy. Every new technology innovation is both a source of deep pleasure and a significant tool in my own evolution.*

Stance 3: Heroic Resistor
While there are clearly some benefits to these new technologies, on the whole they have more negatives than positives. The key is to resist and find ways to

create opportunities and enclaves of non-technological reading, exploration of nature, etc.

*Representative Survey Response:*
*We do not participate in social media other than e-mail. It is just a mindless time-suck.*

Stance 4: Educated Consumer
No technology is inherently good or bad. It requires the considered judgment of a parent or teacher to analyze technology in ever-changing, unique contexts. (COM)

*Representative Survey Response:*
*There are a lot of great resources for the whole family and I find technology often speeds up response time so I don't have to talk on the phone.*

Stance 5: Moderator
In the tradition of Maimonides and Aristotle, moderation is best. Let's figure out the place of technology in our lives and balance it with the other worthwhile things we would like for ourselves and our children.

*Representative Survey Response:*
*I think technology has complicated life but if you don't keep up for your children or yourself, you get left behind. It certainly is a form of entertainment but also a useful tool if used responsibly.*

What stance mirrors your understandings and relationships to technology? One would expect—even hope—that as readers journey through the volume they will move inside each of these perspectives, developing their own unique stances about technology and their Jewish/ethical selves. (COM)

## COMMENTARY

*From Rabbi David Teutsch:* Since writing on Shabbat is forbidden according to Jewish tradition, observant Jews do not touch writing implements such as pencils and pens on Shabbat. Avoiding those objects is not only about avoiding temptation; it is also about keeping away from the objects that will remind us of our workaday concerns. Shabbat is an entirely different experience for those who put away their cellphones, computers, and other electronic devices for Shabbat, saving the time for direct personal interaction and restful activity. The fence demarcates a holy space.

*From Rabbi Nathan Kamesar:* On a good day, I consider myself in this camp. Let's not forget that a book is a piece of technology, a vaccine is a piece of technology, the computer on which this book was no doubt written is a piece of technology. So, too, is a bomb, sarin gas, a lawn mower, and countless other products of human innovation. Just as we can distinguish between these examples, we can distinguish between various applications of twenty-first century digital technologies. A smartphone helps me get navigate the world. Google Glass, a pair of glasses meant to augment what we see, fizzled before it really got off the ground. Let's not paint all technology with the same brush.

*From Dr. Adina Newberg:* In describing Jerusalem Yehuda Amichai talks about the various elements that create divisions in a city, which also help distinguish the many aspects of its life. This description of flow of energy and life can fit the description of fully lived lives in which many elements are intertwined. We can't have a vibrant city or life without distinguishing the flags, the piers and the worship places, but we also know that all of them create a psalm of praise:

*She is always arriving, always sailing away.*
*And the fences and the piers*
*and the policemen and the flags and the high masts of churches*
*and mosques and the smokestacks of synagogues and the boats*
*of psalms of praise and the mountain-waves.*
*The shofar blows: another one*
*has just left*

Amichai's Jewish father and Arab Shepherd know they live in separate spaces, but their cry comes together in the same valley. They are separate, they might be different but their humanity, their laughter and crying transcends the fences created by millennia of fences.

*An Arab shepherd and a Jewish father*
*Both in their temporary failure.*
*Our two voices met above*
*The Sultan's Pool in the valley between us.*

*Afterward we found them among the bushes,*
*And our voices came back inside us*
*Laughing and crying*

*From Rabbi Michael Cohen*: There was a time when our first association with 24-7 was a football score, now it is how we describe the pace of our lives. We are no longer trained, we are no longer given permission, to pause and reflect. In addition, earbuds cut us off from the sounds of the world we live in—the calling of a flock of geese in migration, the crackling of ice in a glass, the gears of a bike and the other subtle sounds from the symphony of our lives, not to mention the person who may be sitting right next to us. Why have we decided that a call from a cell phone trumps a conversation with a person that we are talking to face to face? Why is cell phone interruptus considered to be OK?

*From Rabbi Steve Sager:* Especially with increasing stimuli, we try to be aware of our "fence-off" responses, some of which might surprise us. The Hebrew poet, Zelda, was surprised by her own reaction to a Jerusalem beggar-woman who offered her the gift of a small jar of honey:

*for I had to shatter seven walls of refusal*
*to be able to accept from her hand*
*honey offered as a gift of friendship.*
    (Zelda, "In The Shade Of The Oak")

*From Amelia Gavurin:* Technology is on its way to encouraging or at least allowing us to create fences between ourselves and different aspects of it. Engineers are creating software that makes tech seemingly aware of both self and user. Apple, for instance, now has screen-time reports that show how long a user was on any given app/genre of apps. The software confronts the user with the reality of time spent on their phone and gives them the option to either put up a fence, or ignore. Users can set limits on certain apps or app categories, but they are also allowed to "ignore" those boundaries they set. Just as one can create strict rules for *kashrut* or Shabbat, one can now do the same with technology. In the end though, with technology it comes down to one's willpower, whereas with religion following or not following the rules relies heavily on belief and faith.

## NOTES

1. Two hundred thirty seven parents with children age 2 to 16 responded to a survey by the Jewish Education Center of Cleveland about their own and their childrens' use of technology. (The survey itself can be accessed through Marlyn Jaffe of the

Jewish education center of Cleveland). The results of the survey helped guide the next stage of the project which was developing family education programs. We learned

1). For most of our parents, technology is an organic, patterned part of their lives;

2). There is a concern that technology leads to too much individual and "parallel play" within the family system. Quality family time is sometimes diluted or compromised;

3). While there is a fairly high awareness of what resources exist on the web and in social media in general, the awareness of Jewish resources for learning and home celebration is quite low (for instance only 2% of parents surveyed were aware of the My Jewish Learning website);

4). Voices indicating a "shadow" side to the natural and organic relationship to technology that suggests frustration that technology is a tool that drives them and their children rather than their guiding the applications of technology;

5). There are developmental shifts suggested in the results: with younger children the concern is the "undeveloped" self being exploited in some way by being exposed to developmentally inappropriate materials; as children become young adults the shift is to how the developing internal resources of the child might move in a negative direction through the teens own initiative (presentation of self on media). Concerns about keeping children psychologically safe on the internet are significant but not the dominant concern of parents of teens and tweens.

The survey also framed what became the major project refrain of *Text Me: Ancient Jewish Wisdom Meets Contemporary Technology.* An essential paradox of Jewish parents relationship to technology is that arguably they simultaneously under and over utilize technology. Only 3% of the parents surveyed were aware of the many resources for Jewish parenting and family living on the internet. On the other hand, they admit to more time plugged into general digital resources than they deem healthy for themselves.

2. Chris Argyris and Donald Schon focuses on reflective practice in personal, educational and organizational life. One of the phenomenon they have documented extensively is the gap between our "espoused theories" and our "theories in use". Often "espoused theories reflect our ideals and the values we hold. "Theories in use" pertain to our actions in the world. The gap between the two is often troubling. Aligning these values and actions is challenging work. In regard to the study and more broadly the book the possibility we entertain is that while parents and adults may profess one set of values for their children about technology their own actions themselves are greatly influenced by technology that make it harder for them to serve as role models. The parent who chides his child about too much time with their digital lives as they themselves answer a text is perhaps the paradigmatic example of this concern.

Dear Evolving Self (Dear Jeffrey, Dear Commentator),

*Chapter Three*

# Second Master Text: Two (or Four) Notes in Our Pockets

**BALANCE**, self-awareness, perspective

The second midrash is Chasidic and attributed to the late eighteenth century Hasidic master Rabbi Simcha Bunem It is much quoted around the time of the High Holidays: Human beings need two pockets in the design of their pants or skirts for reasons well beyond matters of style. In one pocket a note reminds us that we are little lower than the angels; I am so important that the world was made on my behalf. In the other pocket a note reads (from the book of *Ecclesiastes* in the Hebrew Bible), human beings are but dust and ashes. Presumably, the dialectical tension between self-awareness and esteem, on the one hand, and deep humility, on the other, sets the stage for teshuvah, the drama of change, forgiveness, and renewal so dramatically embodied in the experience of Rosh Hashanah and Yom Kippur.

My teaching of eighth graders at the Heilicher Minneapolis Jewish Day School convinced me that this folksy yet theologically rich tale, begged for a second set of notes to bring the tale into the digital age. I had spent several months working with eighth graders helping them develop a personal *brit*/covenant focused on their uses of technology. One day one of the students asked me with an absolutely straight face, "Rabbi Jeff, are you anti-technology?"

There is a personal side of my emphatic response of "No I am not anti-technology." Recently, I have felt fortunate that a very dear cousin is likely to survive her battle with cancer, following the most advanced form of proton radiation therapy available at the Mayo Clinic. Almost a dozen years ago, when my sister was dying of cancer she desperately wanted to hear the voices of her family members joined together. Family members for their part wanted to pray for a miraculous recovery. We planned a healing service where we could all pray, laugh, and cry together courtesy of a free conference call service. How could I be anything but "pro" technology when I think of these stories?

Still, my student's comment brought me up short and left me feeling a bit dismayed. It made me aware that I may have given mixed messages to my students. I was challenged to clarify the subtle differences between terms such as criticism, doubt, ambiguity, and perhaps most of all, paradox. For indeed the message I hoped to convey is that we simultaneously and somewhat paradoxically both under and over use technology. Along one dimension, this corresponds to our lack of creativity in utilizing the resources for Jewish living and learning presently available, and digital opportunities to engage in *tikun olam*/world repair, improvement, and transformation. On the other side of the spectrum lie the horror stories of astronomical hours devoted to screen time and frightening tales of cyberbullying.

As a response to my own surprise at failing to communicate my guiding assumption regarding this paradox, I developed a new instructional prop. I now have a pair of pants that I keep around whenever I am queried by a student about my own attitude about technology. The pants, an old pair of jeans, have four pockets with one note in each pocket. The notes in the front two pockets come from the Chasidic teaching discussed above The back pockets contain notes with a technological spin:

#1 Remember: Human beings are made of dust and return to the dust

#2 Remember: You are made just a little lower than the angels; you are God-like

#3 Remember: Human and Jewish life can be made spiritually, intellectually, and ethically so much richer with digital resources

#4 Remember: Your devices and new technologies can do harm as well as good; they can distract from your Godly work

The larger story of how to balance these notes to oneself is addressed throughout the book and particularly in chapters nine and ten where my work with eighth graders at the Heilicher Minneapolis Jewish Day School is presented in more detail.


## COMMENTARY


*From Dr. Terri Elton:* Keeping all four of these notes in dialogue with one another and with our deepest selves is another way of seeing the purpose of this volume.

Dear Evolving Self (Dear Jeffrey, Dear Commentator),

## Chapter Four

# *Pardes,* Judaism, Complexity and Technology: The Orchard of Our Relationship to Technology

**SELF-AWARENESS**, balance, perspective

Judaism has many tools for understanding complexity and paradox. One of them is a methodology of creative interpretation known as *pardes*/orchard or paradise, but also an acronym for *Peshat*/plain meaning, *Remez*/mystical meaning, *Derash*/moral meaning, and *Sod*/philosophical meaning. Any given concept or value can be understood in at least these four different ways depending on which interpretive tool is being utilized.

In this chapter we will try to understand our relationship to technology through the prism of the first three contributing letters of the *pardes* acronym (plain meaning, mystical meaning and moral meaning). The final letter and dimension *sod*/philosophical meaning is presented in Chapter Five. The *resh* and *dalet* are inverted from their place in the acronym because the author believes the moral meaning-making dimension of *derash* psychologically precedes the more soulful introspection of *remez* (mystical meaning). COM

*Peshat:* Plain Meaning
We begin with *peshat,* the relatively observable surface of our relationship to technology. The readers might complete the following sentence stems in considering their relationship to technology *(TMW)*:

My most brilliant use of technology is:

I feel in control of my devices when:

I feel my devices control me when:

My most frustrating experience with technology is:

The difference between my parents and me (or my child and me) in regard to technology is:

I am amazed the way technology helps me:

Technology squeezes out other worthwhile activities when:

My family usually becomes annoyed with me when I use my:

These sentence triggers form a snapshot of our present life in relationship to technology at a given moment. This picture is static, rather than dynamic. It would be helpful then to add some detail that reflects the readers' relationship to technology over time. Even *peshat,* the simplest level of the acronym, has a backstory. Here it is the reader's biography rendered through a technique developed by Dr. Ira Progoff as part of his "At a Journal Workshop" series (Pogroff, 1975, 140) The approach can help add dimensionality and texture to the portrait of our relationship to technology.[1]

Dr. Progoff's technique is built on three unfinished sentences related to the story of our relationship to technology. The first and last statements appear only once: "At first" and "And now." "At first" is our first memory of becoming intrigued or consciously aware of an aspect of technology, often a new (for us) invention. "And now" is how we would describe our relationship to technology at this moment in time, perhaps what most pleases or troubles us about that relationship. Between "At first" and "And now" may flow any number of "And then" statements. (*TMW*)

To make this all concrete enough for the reader to tell his own story, I present aspects of the story of my relationship to technology. This abbreviated sketch does not include all the "And thens" that would constitute the lengthy middle chapters of the book called "Me and Technology."

At first I remember being amazed at the "winky dink" screen placed on my television that allowed me to write on top of the projected television image.

And then I remember the joys of a mahogany brown console radio which allowed me to listen to Sergeant Preston of the Canadian Royal Mounted Police and Dragnet as I lay in bed on Sunday night.

And then I remember how transistor radios allowed me to circumvent my parents' bedtime rule and listen to hockey games at 9:00 in the evening.

And then I remember some thirty years later our first family computer.

And then I began experiencing the travails of a digital immigrant, laboring my way through new technologies of cell phone, laptop, and smartphone, trying to master the new technologies with dated templates of how old toys were put together, constantly searching, as it were for a printed manual in place of the now digitally stored and intuitively guided instructions.

And then as I began to feel more comfortable and competent to experiment with the "world in my hand" of the smartphone and found myself constantly requesting information from Siri about any item or discussion that required information not on my mental hard-drive.

And now I find myself writing this volume—weighing for myself—and encouraging my readers to do the same—the pluses and minuses of the impact of digital technologies on our lives.

Striking the same encouraging note to personalize ideas, the reader is now encouraged to retell personal stories of their own relationship to technology, using these three prompts of At first, And then (multiple entries), And now.

## DERASH: MORAL MEANING AND PERSONAL STANCE

Beneath the surface of our relationship to technology lies an elusive moral dimension. Drill down, and the raw experiences that lie on the surface drop into a well of moral meaning-making. Let's explore this from three different angles. The first comes out of the "six word novel" technique of meaning making. The tradition is often (but perhaps apocryphally) attributed to Ernest Hemingway, whose response to a challenge to write a six-word novel led to the dark, enigmatic FOR SALE: BABY SHOES, NEVER WORN. The New Yorker columnist Larry Smith (Smith, 2006) and others have turned six word novels into something of a cottage industry, a form of "edutainment" designed to be both funny and enlightening. (*TMW).

Below are six word novels created (and reproduced with their and their parents' permission) by students at Heilicher Minneapolis Jewish Day School about their relationship to technology. Readers are invited to review the list and think about which of these seems troubling? Insightful? Profound?

Technology is fun but not too much.

It is changing our lives today.

Technology keeps me connected with friends.

A resource that provides good entertainment.

It's sometimes like a safety blanket.

I use it mostly for doing homework.

It makes things faster and entertains

Technology often helps me procrastinate.

Technology is good but destroying generations.

Technology is helpful but also dangerous

Readers are now invited to boldly and creatively try their hands at developing their own six word novel about technology, perhaps returning to their "And now" statement from the Ira Progoff activity.

Another strategy for exploring the complexity of the role of technology in our lives is to imagine the extremes on a continuum. At one end think of a website such as *Caring Bridge*, where the capacity of a community to love and support an individual going through a health crisis is filtered digitally through the real needs of the family or individual. Clearly, this is an example of *hakarat hatov*/acknowledging the good that technology can do in our lives.

Now imagine the other extreme. Picture someone spending many hours in front of their own screen. This scenario might play out positively if the hours are spent in one of a variety of engaging social simulation games available online. Arguably, it is quite another story if the aim is to achieve some form of complete mindlessness. In some sense this negative scenario reflects the rabbinic concept of *bitul zeman*/wasting our precious resource of time. We will explore this in greater depth in chapter five. (*TMW*)

Now, try to imagine all the gray that lies between the black and white of "technology bad" and "technology good." Try naming half dozen or so examples of gray, where the reader is genuinely conflicted about whether a particular use of technology is neither transparently good or bad, black or white. What accounts for the "grayness?"

1.

2.

3.

4.

5.

6.

Finally, take a look at the graph below, a tool for exploring and categorizing one's own digital habits. It was developed as a *cheshbon hanefesh*/soul inventory instrument for the High Holidays, but is available for our use anytime we are trying to gather our moral bearings in relationship to technology. *(TMW) (COM)*

| Absolute Digital Necessities for work and family | Activities that are diversions from more worthwhile activities |
|---|---|
| Fun, "harmless" forms of entertainment | No No's...better to remove these digital behaviors in the coming year |

## *REMEZ:* TRACES, MYSTERY, AND MUSAR

Our digital lives leave an imprint on both our *guf*/body and *neshamah*/soul. We now know that there is a biochemical phenomenon triggered by the release of dopamine into our bodies. Dopamine feels very, very good. It is associated with sex, chocolate, and, most relevant to our conversation, the ping signaling an incoming email or text. All of these cravings need to be embraced, sanctified, moderated, suppressed, sublimated, or eliminated. (COM)

The journalist Adam Alter, in his provocative volume *Irresistible* makes the case that various forms of screen time qualify as behavioral addictions (Alter, 2017, 1–7) They leave biochemical residues that become congealed into repetitive habit.

We rarely choose these behaviors rationally. The very neuroplasticity of our brains makes us subject to their power. Perhaps most interesting and disturbing to this writer was Alter's discussion of the relationship between evening screen time and sleeplessness. It turns out that the emissions of light from our smartphones is a signal to our brain to wake up. *It is morning* for our brains even when it is indeed the middle of the night. This waking up suppresses the production of the melatonin which is the body's ally in creating our most restful sleeping patterns. A new technology has led to a less disruptive form of light but the temptation to interrupt sleep to work or play remains strong.

The larger point is that we human beings are indeed creatures of habit and making sure that these habits are good ones requires ethical and spiritual effort. *Musar* classes and support groups, which have recently become ubiquitous, can provide a model for creating a curriculum that strives for moral and spiritual completeness in the way they bring *middot*/character traits to awareness.

The tools of the Musar movement are critical allies in charting the *remazim*, the mysteries of who we are and what we are becoming. In Alan Morinis' volume *Everyday Holiness,* twenty-six *midot* are outlined (Morinis, 2017, VII). Seven of them have particularly strong relationships to our digital lives. (*TMW*)

*Anavah*/Humility

Occupy a rightful space, neither too large nor too small. Focus neither on your own virtues nor on the faults of others.

How do you understand the claim that a smartphone puts the world in the palm of your hand?

*Savlanut*/Patience

Whatever may obstruct me from reaching my goals, it is possible to bear the burdens of the situation.

What visceral assumptions do you make when someone has not responded to an email or text in a timely way?

Can I accept the reality that it may not be possible to "keep on top of" my messages and answer each one in a timely way? Can I set an "auto-away" message and accept a period of time when do not act on the impulse to respond? Can I exercise the *middah* of Seder and prioritize my email and texts according to their actual level of urgency?

*Hakarat hatov*/Gratitude

Awaken to the good and give thanks for it.

Do I take for granted the countless nisim shebhol yom asah imanu/the countless miracles of good communication facilitated by digital life?

*Hesed*/Graciousness

Can I give each person the benefit of the doubt (following the rabbinic adage *dan et kol adam l'chaf zechut*, judge each person according to merit), and assume the writer's best intention, rather than the worst?

*Histapkut*/Simplicity

Be satisfied with one's portion and position in life

Does the easy availability of online shopping make my life more efficient or more complicated (or both?)

*Shetikah*/Silence

Nothing soothes nor is better than silence.

When I unplug do I fill my life with other kinds of noises?

*Emet*/Truth

Keep distant from falsehood.

Do I ever exaggerate to enhance my social media profile?

Do I investigate the truth of what I read or post, or simply pass it on without considering its source? Do I avoid investigating the potential truth of views expressed online which may differ from my own?

*Shvil hazahav*/Moderation

Awareness allows me to observe the pull of impulse and then provides wisdom to guide the response.

On the whole do I feel well balanced in my uses of technology?

The number four has special Jewish potency as it is associated with the four questions asked at the Passover *seder*. In that spirit the reader might consider these four broader questions:

Is this *midah* one of ethical strength or weakness in my own moral makeup?

In what ways do I embody the positive side of the *midah*? In what ways is it challenged or undermined by my everyday routine?

What enters my life digitally (smartphone, computer, social media) that either strengthens or challenges my relationship to the *midah?*

When is my spiritual/ethical core shaping my use of technology and when is technology shaping my spiritual/ethical core?

## COMMENTARY

*Rabbi Marc Margolius:* Jewish tradition emphasizes both the possibility and necessity of human moral freedom. The Exodus narrative describes the process of realizing freedom as a manifestation of the Divine, enabling human beings to serve their highest purpose. At the same time, Jewish tradition recognizes that engrained patterns of behavior over time constrain our freedom, restricting our capacity to make wise or holy choices. (The "hardening" of Pharaoh's heart, for example, represents a phenomenon of self-perpetuating obstinacy.) Rabbi Akiba captures this dialectic in his adage that "all is foreseen, and freedom of choice is given" (*Pirkei Avot* 3:19).

In Mussar and the Jewish ethical tradition, the first step in maximizing our potential for freedom, and avoiding the dangers of enslavement or idolatry, is cultivating *da'at* (consciousness), awareness of the fullest range of options available to us, as well as of the obstacles that hinder our freedom. Jewish tradition employs several practices and perspectives for cultivating such awareness: Shabbat, the *Shema*, and *Hineini* ("I am present"). Each of which focuses on cultivating attention to the Presence of the Divine in the present moment. Each of these is designed to help us "stay woke."

Spiritually "waking up," fostering greater awareness of self, environment, and Divine Presence, strengthens our capacity for wise *bechirot* (choices) with regard to technology. Jewish tradition posits as well that we innately possess an array of moral/spiritual qualities known as *middot* (literally, "measures" of each trait) which, applied individually or in combination, can guide us to wiser behavior. Applied consistently, these sacred qualities can help us relate wisely to our technology and enable it to function as a tool by which we increase holiness in the world, rather than as a master or idol to which we become enslaved.

*From Rabbi David Teutsch:* It is far too narrow to limit worthwhile activities, to home/family and work. Most of us use computers in a broad variety of ways in the process of doing mitzvot and volunteer work. We use specialized programs for organizing food deliveries for those who are ill. We use electronic communication and spreadsheets to organize Torah reading assignments. We use accounting software to keep track of our organizations' finances. We use publishing software to produce newsletters. We use listservs to communicate about deaths and shiva minyanim. Good use of computers and social media can help to sustain effective and loving communities. We can also use these tools for studying Torah and doing other forms of research. The positive uses are literally endless.

*From Rabbi Mira Wasserman:* Identifying the four components of PaRDeS as" tools" is helpful in that it invites us to think about them as technology. Peshat, Derash, Remez and Sod are four different modes of interpretation. Traditionally these four interpretive tools are applied to texts of Torah—they are technologies that mediate between the reader and the text. In this sense, they can be compared to electronic media that mediate between users and the world. Each of the four tools of PaRDeS helps us pay attention to a different aspect of a text, highlighting some features and screening out others. In a similar way, mediating technologies like Google, Facebook, and any number of apps give us access to some parts of the world and screen out others. What do your media highlight? What do they leave out? How do you align your media tools with the aspects of life you want to attend to?

Peshat, Derash, Remez and Sod are tools for interpreting the texts of Torah. The antiquity of the written text of the Torah means that it does not directly address electronic technology, but many verses of the Torah relate to the themes and questions raised in this book.

Here are two key verses that invite interpretation in light of this book's themes: "Listen, Israel, Adonai is our God, Adonai alone." (Deut 6:4) "See, this day I set before you blessing and curse." (Deut 11:26)

*From Rabbi Nathan Kamesar:* No doubt! In many ways, the need to self-regulate our technology usage can be thought of similarly to our need to exercise. Transitioning from the ancient ways of hunting and gathering to today's labor specialization and market economies leads, for many, to far more sedentary lifestyles. Thus, on our best days we supplement our lives with a good exercise regimen. Use of technology works similarly. In the same ways that we wouldn't want to go back to a hunter-gatherer lifestyle but also want to make sure to re-introduce some physical exercise into our lives, we don't (or

I don't) want to go back to a screen-free lifestyle but to want to reintroduce periods of calm and quiet into my life.

This is in some ways the fundamental question when it comes to our use of technology. When are we allowing it to take hold of us in subtle ways that, because of its ubiquity in our life, sneak up on us and take control of our way of being? And when do we exhibit conscientiousness and discernment, such that technology facilitates our learning and exploring rather than insidiously manipulating us into indolence or depravity.

## NOTE

1. Donald Schon and Chris Agrys have partnered on numbers of books about the role of reflective practice in management, industry, and education. The most comprehensive presentation of their joint theories is in Organizational Learning II (Reading, Massachussetts: Addison and Weseley Publishing 1996.)

Dear Evolving Self (Dear Jeffrey, Dear Commentator),

## Chapter Five

# *Sod*/The Spiritual and Philosophical Core

**PERSPECTIVE,** balance, self-awareness

*Sod*/foundation speaks to the intellectual, spiritual, and philosophical foundations of who we are. It is the big picture of our lives that so often escapes us
when we are wrapped up in everyday details. In the twenty-first century these
foundations are particularly fluid and dynamic.The ideational threads are
often wrapped together so tightly that we need an almost revelatory experience to see these dimensions clearly and distinctly.

Our relationship to digital life is embedded in a lattice of larger assumptions about human beings and their relationship to tools and technology. Even
as we place the world in our hands with our smartphones, there is a world
within us that interprets what such a powerful tool means to us. We need to
play what Stephen Brookfield calls "the assumption hunting game" to flesh
out these assumptions (Brookfield, 2017, 5–10)(COM)

To sensitize ourselves to the multiplicity of our potential views about
technology from a Jewish perspective, I have placed below three short statements related to the Jewish Sabbath. These will help us utilize the worldviews
of Abraham Joshua Heschel, Mordecai Kaplan, and Joseph Soloveitchik to
deepen our exploration of how technology plays a role in shaping our exis-
tential selves.[1]

Abraham Joshua Heschel, *The Sabbath,* (prologue):

He who wants to enter the holiness of the day must first lay down the profan-
ity of clattering commerce, of being yoked to toil. He must go away from the
screech of dissonant days, from the nervousness and fury of acquisitiveness and
the betrayal in embezzling his own life. He must say farewell to manual labor
and learn to understand that the world has already been created and will survive

without the help of man. Six days a week we wrestle with the world, wringing profit from the earth; on the Sabbath we especially care for the seed of eternity planted in the soul. The world has our hands, but our soul belongs to Someone Else. Six days a week we seek to dominate the world, on the seventh day we try to dominate the self.

## Mordechai M. Kaplan, *The Meaning of God in Modern Jewish Religion* (chapter on Sabbath)

In pursuit of other aims we frequently become so absorbed in the means as to lose sight of the goal.... Here the Sabbath comes to our aid. An artist cannot be continually wielding his brush. He must stop at times in his painting to freshen his vision of the object, the meaning of which he wishes to express on his canvas.

Living is also an art. We dare not become absorbed in its technical processes and lose our consciousness of its general plan....The Sabbath represents those moments when we pause in our brushwork to renew our vision of the object. Having done so we take ourselves to our painting with clarified vision and renewed energy.

## Joseph B. Soloveitchik, *The Lonely Man of Faith, chapter 2:*

Adam I

...dignity was equated by the Psalmist with man's capability of dominating his environment and exercising control over it. Man acquires dignity through glory, through his majestic posture vis-à-vis his environment.

[This] dignity cannot be realized as long as he has not gained mastery over his environment. [It is through rational, logical, and mathematical operations that this mastery begins to unfold.] Man of old who could not fight disease and succumbed in multitudes to yellow fever or any other plague with degrading helplessness could not lay claim to dignity. Only the man who builds hospitals, discovers therapeutic techniques, and saves lives is blessed with dignity...

To conquer space, he boards a plane at the New York airport at midnight and takes several hours later a leisurely walk along the streets of London.... Man of the seventeenth and eighteenth centuries who needed several days to travel from Boston to New York was less dignified than a man whose mastery has made it possible for him to act in accordance with his responsibility... the Biblical promise of being creatures b'tzelem elohim made in the image of God.

Adam II is different

He looks for the image of God not in the mathematical formula or the natural relational law but in every beam of light, in every bud and blossom, in the morning breeze and still of a starlit evening. In a word, Adam the second explores not the scientific abstract universe but the irresistibly fascinating qualitative world where he establishes an intimate relation with God.

Here are some questions we might pose relative to these portraits:
Beyond the Sabbath, which of the three reflects the most positive appreciation of the role technology plays in our lives?
Conversely, which has the most negative view?
How would each have us evaluate the impact of technology on our lives? (*TMW*)

Of course these quotations are merely the ripples of deeper currents of thought running through the three thinkers. Going deeper reveals additional complexity. Perhaps, Heschel provides the most consistent message. His equation of technology with the conquest of space stands in stark contrast with the "palace of time" that is the Sabbath. Though he clearly recognizes that one must live in technical civilization as well, ("Six days shall you labor..."), the Sabbath remains the prize. Heschel notes that in the liturgical poem *Lehah Dodi* which welcomes the Sabbath as a bride and queen, the Sabbath is praised, "first (in God's thoughts) though last in creation." It transcends the rest of creation because in some sense it is the purpose of creation. (COM)

Yet Heschel acknowledges multiple paths to discovering God's presence in the world. Labor is one thing if it is in service of more skyscrapers and monuments. It is quite another if during the six days of labor we are addressing issues of social justice and human harmony. These are deep and passionate concerns of Heschel. Famously, one engages in the prototypical Sabbath act of prayer with one's feet ("I felt as if my feet were praying," he said as he marched alongside Martin Luther King in Selma, Alabama in 1965 for the civil rights of African-Americans).

Arguably, one needs to turn to another of Heschel's volumes to understand his views on our relationship to technology. *The Earth is the Lord's* is Heschel's tribute to life in seventeenth and eighteenth century Eastern Europe. A reviewer of the volume notes that Heschel assiduously avoids any reference to the physical architecture of the buildings of the time. It is all about the spiritual architecture of the Ashkenazi world that is his spiritual home. It seems fair to say that Heschel's worldview is not anti-technology, but rather, transcends it. The material world—so much the body of technology—is of minimal interest to him (Byron, 2007)

This provides quite a strong contrast to the work of Soloveitchik. At first glance, one might say that Soloveitchik represents a pro-technology stance, given his exuberant praise of Adam I's achievements in the realms of math, science, and technology (remember that he flies from Boston to

London in a few short hours rather than trudging step by step to his intended destination).

In teaching Soloveitchik in various settings I have noticed how easily he can be interpreted as the embodiment of a problematic hubris, the elevation of human beings above the rest of creation. Arguably, this elevation leaves the natural world open to subjugation, rape, and pillage. Admittedly, there are structures of Jewish and civil law mitigating the use of this power. Yet the very placement of humanity on the highest rung of the chain of being can remain problematic. Famously in 1967 a group of theologians (none Jewish) meeting at Claremont College laid the impending environmental crisis at the foot of the twenty eighth verse of the first chapter of Genesis and the Judaeo-Christian tradition that views human beings as empowered by God to conquer and subdue the natural world.

In the interest of balance, one needs to recognize the dialectic nature of Soloveitchik's views of human origins, purpose, and destiny. Adam II is created out of the very elements of the natural world. He embraces that world as a source of inspiration, apparently with no interest in conquering it.

The intricate, reciprocal relationship between Adam I and II is captured by Soloveitchik in one of final chapters of *The Lonely Man of Faith:*

> The Biblical dialectic stems from the fact that Adam the first, majestic man of dominion and success and Adam the second, the lonely man of faith, obedience and defeat are not two different people locked in an external confrontation as an I opposite a thou, but one person who is involved in self-confrontation...God created two Adams and sanctioned both. Rejection of either aspect of humanity would be tantamount to an act of disapproval of the divine scheme of creation.

Soloveitchik recognizes that this dialectical tension can easily be thrown out of kilter. He notes near the end of the volume the crude and crass materialism that might be confused with Adam I's mission in mid-twentieth century life. On the other hand, one senses he would have had little sympathy for the metaphoric hugging of trees that arguably strips Adam I entirely of his dominance over nature. A colleague and student of Soloveitchik once quipped that eventually Soloveitchik comes to favor Adam I because the skills of logic and technical mastery best equip people to engage in Talmudic study. (COM)

Mordecai Kaplan falls in the middle of a continuum that can be constructed—at least for heuristic purposes—as having Soloveitchik and Heschel representing the pro and anti-technology points along the spectrum. Kaplan is a philosophical pragmatist and likely to be found in the middle on any number of issues. He sees the value of technology in the uses to which we put it. It is a means to an end. (COM)

Kaplan's sense of balance leads him to remark about technology throughout *Not So Random Thoughts* (Kaplan, 1966):

In the present emphasis of "know how" and "know what" we overlook the importance of "know-what-for."

All one needs to do to explode the myth of technology as always positive is to realize without Eli Whitney's invention of the cotton gin in 1794 there never would have been a Civil War.

Similarly he remarks:

Ancient civilization was all ends and no means
A modern civilization is all means and no end.

This last remark seems to mirror a constant lament of Einstein that we have a plethora of means (technical skills) and a dearth of wisdom about how to deploy them. Yet this is the same Mordecai Kaplan who as a child marveled at the new uses of technology demonstrated at the Paris World's Fair in 1900 (Scult, 2002) Further, in an excerpt from his diaries Kaplan takes deep issue with his colleagues' opinion that technology could be ultimately at odds with Judaism. The presenting issue in the diary excerpt: The number of Jews who stayed home to watch the international premier of Peter Pan on television rather than attend Purim services.

This attitude frustrated and angered many of Kaplan's Conservative colleagues, but for him the enduring challenge was how to revitalize Jewish culture, religion, and civilization through all means possible including technology. There was no room for *kvetching* (complaining) or whining in this vision. The challenge was to do Peter Pan in Hebrew with great technological flare.

So what does it mean to take a pragmatic position about technology in our world of digital abundance? Clearly, it means to engage in something like what, in organizational change and management circles, is called values based decision making. In any given situation the multiple and interactive Jewish and human values at play must be weighed and considered. Any path chosen should reflect the interplay of these values.

Here decision making is neither simple nor binary. A point of contrast with the most traditional views of Jewish learning and purpose might be helpful here. For millennia when a Jew would complete a section of Talmud study he would celebrate with a *khadran*/declaration of intent to return to these very same pages and learn more (and at the same time return to her divine source of inspiration). The language of the *khadran* is paraphrased below in terms of what kind of activities meet the criteria of Jewish purpose and salvation.

*Some people waste their time gambling, hanging around street corners and other blasphemous activities. We (the Jewish people) study your holy Torah and constantly return to this task.*

This view of the purpose of human activity is linked to a Jewish value concept of *bittul zeman*/refraining from activity that is a waste of time (here operationally defined as deflecting us from Torah study). It is precisely such a dichotomous position that Kaplan is most likely to reject. Like the philosopher John Dewey from whom he borrows, every ethical decision is an experiment shaped by the consequences of our action.

This suggests a different challenge for our relationship to digital technologies. The key is whether they help fill our lives with worthwhile activities or not. Kaplan creates a high bar for this assessment. Both Judaism and post-modernity have to provide "salvational" opportunities, opportunities to engage in activity that is spiritually the equivalent of the holiness Jews derived from Torah and prayer in their more cloistered pre-modern environments. Certainly creative arts, literature, drama and music are "salvational" within this framework. So too our activities that lead to *tikkun olam*/world improvement and transformation.

When we turn to technology in general and especially digital technology, within this framework, there is, unsurprisingly, great complexity. It is possible that some of the uses of screen time are ethically neutral (or even positive), yet still divert us from more worthwhile activities. One takes seriously for instance the work of Richard Louv, *Last Child in the Woods: Saving Our World from Nature-Deficit Disorder (Louv, 2005,* Introduction*)* If the digital world displaces, rather than supplements, our time in the natural world it is a cause of deep concern.

Though the previous analysis is focused on the individual, the application of philosophical pragmatism also applies to the community. Synagogues need to develop positions about their relationship to technology. Often this has to do with permitted or forbidden use of various forms of technology on Shabbat and holidays.

Consider this tale of three synagogues where I have made presentations about Judaism and technology. In one, the professional staff told me that it was fine and good to go through some process of values based decision making so long as it ended up permitting the use of their smartphones and other devices. They could not imagine being without their phones for personal or professional uses on Shabbat. Conversely, in one of the shuls that I belong to there is a weekly reminder to turn off your smartphones in order to protect the sanctity of the Shabbat. But in a third—I imagine more reflective of the majority of liberal synagogues in North America—things are a bit up in the air.

Here is where Kaplanian pragmatism seems to be most helpful. Below are I present a number of possible uses of a smartphone on Shabbat. Examining the specific personal and societal contexts in which philosophical principles are at play is at the heart of philosophical pragmatism. It allows the possibility of the ideal and the real entering into dialogue with one another and generating more vibrant and meaningful principles to guide the community in their decision making. (*TMW*).

## Potential Uses of a Smart Phone on Shabbat

Rank order these potential uses of a smartphone on Shabbat from most permissible to least permissible within your own values framework:

____ Finding relevant resources related to machlokot/divisions of opinion that occur during a Torah study session.
____ Completing an urgent piece of business not completed during the week.
____ Calling 911 when a congregant has a heart attack.
____ Placing a bet on the Sunday's football game.
____ Watching a Jewish movie.
____ Making sure that a playdate for a child is still on later that afternoon.
____ Playing a most amazing new tune of the Maccabeats for Chanukah.
____ Responding to a text from a long estranged relative.

A group exploring this dilemma might also discuss whether there should be unplugged zones in the synagogue that are space dependent (rather than time, Shabbat dependent). Are there types of synagogue functions (study, spirituality groups)) where the agreed upon norm is that phones are collected before the activity begins?

To be successfully executed these opening dialogues must be followed by a series of thoughtful activities, reflections, and clarifications that can lead to a policy that passes the dual pragmatic impulses of being both principled and reflective of the real needs of a given community.

It might be useful to contrast such a search for process and guiding principles with a different kind of adaptation, a pure compromise between the demands of the digital world and the Jewish tradition. Such a compromise is found in the emerging traditions of "half Shabbat " in the Modern Orthodox world where among millennials texting is a considered a permitted activity while all other halachic prescriptions are maintained. As opposed to an acceptable compromise, values based decision making might guide the community towards a principled contextualism where decisions are based on prized and cherished values in real time and in complex circumstances. One might even arrive at some of the same practices but through a very different process.

## COMMENTARY

*From Elliot Dorff:* Yet, Heschel acknowledges multiple paths to discovering God's presence in the world." Early in his book, *God in Search of Man* (p. 31), he writes that we come to know God in three ways—"in the world, in things"; through "sensing His presence in the Bible'"; and though "sensing His presence in sacred deeds"—and the book is divided into those three sections. We can come to know God in these ways, however, only if we pursue them in particular ways. Specifically, in the world of things we must recognize the sublime, mystery, and glory of the world to lead us, respectively, to wonder, awe, and faith. Learning will lead us to God only if we understand that that the Torah itself is a *midrash* (interpretation) of our ancestors' experiences with God, ones that we can repeat and use for ourselves. He thinks, though, that the most effective way of knowing God is through fulfilling the commandments, assuming that we do so not in a mechanistic way but with the intent to connect to God through them. "These three ways correspond in our tradition to the main aspects of religious existence: worship; learning, and action" (p. 31).

*Rabbi David Teutsch:* Torah study and prayer remain paths to holiness for many of us. And our ancestors certainly experienced uplift from music, dance, celebration and fulfilling mitzvot that help others. We contemporary folks tend to make far too sharp a line between what worked for our ancestors and what works for us. Rabbi Mordecai Kaplan's use of "salvation" is meant as a criterion by which any conduct can be assessed. Does it uplift? Does it bring enhanced awareness of the Divinity infused in the world? Does it better people's lives? That is the path of Torah, the path of salvation. When things become rote or emptied of content, or they are activities that lead us to less integrity or less caring or less sensitivity, they lead us away from salvation. These questions about salvation can be raised about any activity, including those involving electronic devices. Does this activity add meaning? Does it serve others? Is it a source of salvation?

*Rabbi Nathan Kamesar:* This can evoke either a nihilist response (what does it matter what I do?) or one marked by humility (my effect on the world is slight but precious). How we respond to this insight—that the world will survive without our help—is a reflection of our faith, our tradition, and our values. Pressing pause, as the recalling of Shabbat implores us to do, is an expression of our Jewishness.

*From Dr. Terri Elton*: Technology is not easily reduced to function but is more complex and integrated into all aspects of life. Simplifying technology to one or two aspects reduces this complexity and the contribution it has personally and communally to our well-being. The greater, or deeper, issue is our human need for sabbath and wondering how digital tools distract us from ourselves, our primary relationships, and God.

*From Rabbi Michael Cohen:* Lynn White in his famous essay, *The Historical Roots of Our Ecologic Crisis* (1967), places the blame on the twenty-eighth verse of the Bible. He and others forgot to read in the next chapter (2:15) where we are told to, "till and guard," the environment. White and others are selective in their reading of the text while Soloveitchik presents a fuller and more complex reading and message.

Kaplan also said, "As a result of the mechanization and over-industrialism of present-day life, the human being has come to stand in greater need of the Sabbath than ever before...the function of the Sabbath is to prohibit man from engaging in work which in any way alters the environment, so that he should not delude himself into the belief that he is complete master of his destiny."

## NOTE

1. Almost any shortlist of significant Jewish thinkers of the 20th century will include the names of Abraham Joshua Heschel, Rabbi Joseph Soliveitichik, and Mordecai M. Kaplan. Alan Levenson's *Modern Jewish Thinkers* (New York: Rowman and Littlefield, 2006) provides a fine summary of their thought. The selections about the Sabbath are illustrative of their roots in traditions of dialectical philosophy (Soloveitchik), pragmatic philosophy (Kaplan), and depth theology (Heschel).

Dear Evolving Self (Dear Jeffrey, Dear Commentator),

*Part II*

# THE LARGER STORY OF JUDAISM AND TECHNOLOGY

## Chapter Six

# Scratches, Scrolls, Books, and Blogs: The Long History of Judaism's Relationship with Information Technology (Brian Amkraut)

**PERSPECTIVE,** self-awareness, balance

Since the turn of the millennium the educational world (along with most every industry) has been abuzz with the need to respond to the challenges created by a world awash in new technologies. The advent of email, the world-wide-web, social media, machine learning, and ever-changing mobile technologies have indeed radically altered the economic, social, and even political environments in which we operate, and it is hard to find an area which has not been deeply affected by the disruptive forces of our increasingly wired (and wireless) global community. And while Jewish life in its many facets has hardly been immune to these powerful forces, it bears reflection that a 3000 year old religion and civilization has witnessed its share of revolutionary developments in the past, particularly in the realm of information technologies. This brief analysis of the ongoing relationship between Jewish life and its relationship to media should provide a broad context for understanding the challenges of today's digital culture and its implications for the future.

The long view presented here does not focus extensively on the specific details of any particular era, but rather examines the history of Jewish life's relationship with technology by addressing three elements that are critical to understanding the connection between Jewish textual traditions and how the Jewish people relate to those words and concepts. These three overarching issues can be characterized as mutability, accessibility, and authority. Mutability describes the extent to which the specific language of Jewish texts and the traditions they represent can change or be changed in accordance with specific historical contexts. Accessibility addresses the ability of individuals or groups of people to directly engage with the textual tradition which at one time or another represents the received wisdom of the past, whether

49

ascribed to divine authorship or human interpretation. Authority refers to the question of who has the right to explain the implications of those texts and traditions for the lives of individual Jews, and at times to legislate and adjudicate accordingly. Interestingly the changes in media technology over many centuries do not result in a linear development with respect to mutability, accessibility, and authority, but rather tell a more dynamic story, reflecting relationships that seem often to be in flux and tension with one another. Counter-intuitively, some aspects of today's user-based digital culture have more in common with pre- or early-historic modes of transmission than with the ways of the world only a century ago. (COM)

A basic principle of physics is Newton's first law, which states "every object persists in its state of rest or uniform motion in a straight line unless it is compelled to change that state by forces impressed on it." This axiom holds true for historical trends no less than it does for physical objects. Generally speaking, cultural, social, and political environments continue on relatively unchanged until a force emerges causing a change of course. That force may come forth in the form of an individual actor (the so-called great-man theory) or in the form of ideas and inventions which alter the otherwise inertial direction of history. Depending on the nature of the specific force involved, the changes, when they occur, may come rapidly or only unfold over long periods of time. Of equal importance for understanding historical developments is Newton's second law, in abbreviated form, "To every action there is always an equal and opposite reaction." These two pieces of elementary physics frame the story of human historical development, and Jewish history too reflects those basic principles. Taking a traditional starting point such as the giving of the law on Mount Sinai, for example, the Israelite people, left alone and unchecked, would have maintained a strict biblical way of life—as external and at times internal forces—impacted that course of events, so the tradition reacted, and developed into new directions, at times radically different from the trajectory it appeared to have been following. The metaphor of Newtonian physics helps understand the relationship between tradition (both the narrative and legalistic elements of tradition) and technology, whereby invention and innovation behave as impactful forces and the tradition reacts accordingly.

Information technology in particular has critical significance for the transmission of Jewish texts and traditions across generations. To be sure the role that IT plays in this regard is not limited to the digital revolution of the 21st century, but rather the whole notion of Jewish continuity and connection to the Jewish past hinges entirely on the ability to communicate that heritage, both among members of the community at any given point in time, and subsequently between one generation and another. The modes of communication, which have changed over time, directly impact the mutability and accessibility of those traditions, as well as the ability of individuals and groups to exercise authority in that regard. Jewish tradition specifically recognizes the importance of media in transmission, including specific religious commandments to save the divine word in written form, and incorporating a veneration for written text within the very stories that gave rise to Judaism as a distinct civilization.

Looking back to the earliest means of communicating the legacy of Jewish learning, including religious guidance, most scholarship clearly points to an oral transmission predating the first written materials by hundreds of years. And a simple comparison of oral vs. written modalities shows the radical shift that will occur with the emergence of the latter. Oral transmission requires no technology, demands prodigious memory skills but also results in constant editing and revision (both consciously and subconsciously) creating texts and traditions that are inherently fluid but also broadly accessible. Indeed the theatrical and interpretive element of oral transmission could provide compelling cause in its own right to encourage variant tellings of a common story.

The written word demands a medium, whether on cave walls, clay tablets, papyrus, or animal skins. Literacy is obviously a critical skill necessary to participate in the process of written transmission, and the process of putting words into writing creates *de facto* a mechanism for canonization. The early process of manually transcribing written materials, however, created room for both human error in the process of replication as well as editorial license to alter text. Nevertheless the act of transcription as opposed to oral transmission leads to a more static text compared to the dynamism of the spoken word, and the Bible itself explicitly values the written word as more authentic. And here we can see the Newtonian analogy come into play—the written word, specifically the reliance on the Torah as an authoritative text likely resulted in a fundamental shift in the nature of the Israelite religion and worship.

The Bible's depiction of Sinaitic Revelation has the finger of God carving the Ten Commandments into stone—the very phrase "etched in stone" still today purporting both permanence and authority. The Book of Kings describes the young monarch Josiah's encounter with a newly "discovered" scroll of the law found in the royal treasury. According to the Biblical narrative "When the king heard the words of the scroll of the Teaching, he rent his clothes." Josiah and his entourage realize that the mode of worship employed at that time varied from the instructions indicated on the written text they now possessed, "For great indeed must be the wrath of the LORD that has been kindled against us, because our fathers did not obey the words of this scroll to do all that has been prescribed for us" (II Kings 22:11-13). Similarly the story of Ezra the Scribe depicts an encounter between the people and the written word as if for the very first time (as for some it may indeed have been). Following Ezra's reading the ancient text to the Israelites, "The whole community that returned from the captivity made booths and dwelt in the booths—the Israelites had not done so from the days of Joshua son of Nun to that day—and there was very great rejoicing" (Nehemiah 8: 17). While the reaction differs in each case—in the latter instance, joy at the opportunity to worship according to the divine law, as opposed to Josiah's contrition for failing to do so—they both recognize the authority of the written word over any prevailing popular custom. Indeed the very notion of a "People of the Book" may derive from this ultimately broadly accepted notion (even within Christian and Muslim tradition) recognizing the validity of the divine word as transmitted in an authentic written text.

Though the process likely included a number of iterations over many centuries, the original tradition which may have preserved multiple and competing narratives was replaced with a single text and began the process of uniform practice. (Both the biblical text itself and archeological evidence suggest that different modes of worship existed concurrently in ancient Israelite society). At the same time the action of canonizing a written text also resulted in the Newtonian reaction of demanding a process of interpretation and the emergence of a scholarly class (i.e. rabbis) to guide the people in proper adherence to the written code. This shifted authority from Kings and Priests to Rabbis and scholars. While we know very little historically about the impact of the first writing of Jewish texts and the role of scribes as authorities in Jewish life, the corpus of Rabbinic literature and subsequent commentary (collectively often called the Oral Law, see below) provides centuries worth of examples of the power of the written word and the role of those empowered to craft and interpret those words.

With respect to Jewish texts one should be careful not to conflate the notion of oral transmission with the concept of Oral Law. Though one could argue the initial function of Oral Law (interpretive and supplementary material to Biblical texts) was indeed to maintain fluidity and avoid canonization, in reality the proliferation of Oral Law, especially once it too appeared in written form, led to greater consistency and uniformity in the practice of Jewish law and the continuity of traditions. From a technical perspective, however, these materials were also initially transcribed manually and subject to error and revision. The enormous quantity of these Rabbinic tomes further reinforced the exclusivity of access as only a select few had the critical skills and training necessary to fully explore the breadth of these writings and thereby serve as legitimate religious authorities. Comparative analysis to early Christian tradition, as well as internal exegesis of Jewish religious tradition would indicate a clear class distinction on the basis of religious literacy, to the point that the clergy with access and authority had both political and economic motivations to maintain their status. Notions of widespread Jewish literacy in the Rabbinic and Medieval eras are anachronistic; the high expense for and limited access to written materials combined with the desire to maintain rabbinic interpretation of Jewish law and tradition both supported retaining those skills exclusively within the community of scholars. As radical as the rabbinic era of written commentary and interpretation may have been compared to the cultic practices of ancient Israelite worship, so too the transformations ultimately derived from subsequent revolutions in print and then electronic media ushered in vastly different relationships between the Jewish people, religious leadership, and their traditions.

Of course the next major stage of communication technology emerges with the invention of the printing press. While enabling the mass production of written material, Gutenberg's invention could also be seen as a step forward on the path of progress in communication—that is the drive to eliminate human error in the transmission of information. And again some ambiguity emerges in this respect—on the one hand book printing clearly enables replication of materials on a massive scale—but ironically any errors that may have found their way into the printed text will then be transmitted as authentic, possibly without subsequent revision in later generations. Importantly the broader impacts of the printing press, including improved literacy rates and lower production and distribution costs, lead to greater accessibility for these materials. For Jewish texts the printing press stimulated the growth of a culture of book learning, particularly with respect to the Talmud, subsequently increasing the numbers of people who could speak with authority on the content and relevance of those materials. Perhaps unintentionally, however, the emergence of printed texts also created an environment that allowed for challenges to the exclusive authority of any given class to interpret the divine word or even the ability to access news of the world. These consequences likely explain the Catholic Church's eventual opposition to widespread printing, despite an early embrace of the technology as an effective means of spreading the gospel. And while no evidence suggests a parallel Jewish challenge to printed matter, the long-term effects demonstrate similar potential threats to traditional rabbinic dominance. (COM)

The proliferation of printed matter took a number of generations, but ultimately, of course, created a sea change in the mechanism for communication. The example of Martin Luther's role in the Protestant Reformation is a case in point. Luther was neither the first nor the last to criticize the policies and operations of the Catholic Church and in another era his 95 Theses would likely have remained a localized affair. But combine Luther's challenge with Gutenberg's invention and one has the ingredients necessary to foment revolutionary change. These developments, not surprisingly, coincided with the emergence of the Age of Discovery, which allowed and often encouraged challenging received wisdom when it conflicted with reasoned empirical observation. Similarly in the Jewish world, over time, the ease of access to printed materials also enabled challenges to traditional notions of who had authority to interpret those texts, and encouraged new approaches to analyzing both Biblical and Rabbinic materials. Not surprisingly, as we know from current punditry and reactions to later technological developments, social observers and the guardians of morality of that era viewed the emergence and rapid proliferation of printing presses as a scourge on society to be avoided. Of course the scribes themselves were impacted economically, ending an elite profession with possibly 6,000 years of history, but the real challenge appeared in the realm of social control and access to information. In certain respects the critics were correct—the changes were revolutionary (if a 200 year process can be called revolutionary), but as has been the case ever since, once the genie is out of the bottle, it cannot be returned. Consequently, "the authorities," whoever they might be, and indeed the very notion of legitimate tradition, needed to adapt to the reality of this new-fangled technology, as they all ultimately did. Laws of libelous press and copyright infringement (and in some regimes outright censorship) emerged, demonstrating society's attempts to impose a measure of order and to demonstrate communal consensus in an exploding world of access. (COM)

An important outgrowth of print technology in the Jewish world was the enforcement of greater homogeneity of home and communal practice in the Jewish world. Throughout the Middle Ages Jewish communities as far flung as England, Spain, North Africa, and Persia recognized the authority of rabbinic academies, mainly in the Middle East, to interpret, and even legislate for all of world Jewry. Nevertheless, there is clear evidence of regional and even local variation in ritual practice until the early Modern era. This variation reflected not only local communal needs and acculturation to surrounding norms, but also the impracticalities of depending on communication across many miles of land and sea, and the lack of access throughout the Diaspora to authoritative texts. While industrialized printing improved access ultimately enabling challenges to inherited tradition, it also provided a highly effective means of standardization. Mass produced standardized prayer books, and ultimately widely distributed standardized codes of practice (The *Shulchan Aruch* in particular) reduced and sometimes even eliminated regional and local variations in liturgy and ritual.

The more recent "information age" saw important transformations in communications technologies and even in its earlier stages brought radical developments in the relationships between individuals and information. And while these specific technological advancements did not always directly produce corollary changes in Jewish practice and leadership, they all contributed to the normalization of a culture of change in Western Culture further opening the door to further challenges to religious authority and greater access to the textual resources of Judaism. Consider the impacts of the following transitions:

From telegraphy to telephony:

As important as the advent of telegraphy had been, that initial electronic technology was limited in a number of ways. Transmission occurred in code and was mediated by the wire service provider, typically Western Union in the case of the U.S., and generally involved significant time lag (by twentieth-century standards) between the time an initial message was sent and a reply was received. Of course the telegraph greatly reduced the weeks or months such correspondence had previously entailed through the written word (even though the Pony Express had seemed to revolutionize that process). But then compare communication by phone to the telegraph, with the telephone providing instant dialogue, the ability to convey tone and nuance, without the limitations of a Morse code.

From print media, to radio, to television:

Again, while archaic by contemporary standards, the innovation of live broadcast media brought with it not only significant developments in the transmission of information, but those changes were accompanied by important modifications in social patterns. Consider the difference of reading the newspaper at one's leisure, either at home or in a public space, to the centrality of the radio and then television to the daily schedule of family life. The electronic devices soon came to embody the family hearth for 20th century middle-class American families with the transmission of information a passive activity with its content determined by those empowered to craft and offer programming to the general public. Importantly these resources of mass media—newspapers, radio, and television—served as authoritative voices in the modern world, representing a 4th Estate that often saw itself as a bearer of truth, superior in that respect to the old establishments of either church or state. Jewish dependence on received wisdom, even received textual wisdom, suffered alongside its Christian counterparts, as more and more citizens of modern societies depended on the commercial outlets of mass media for guidance. At the emergence of the digital age, text-based religious traditions had already been radically transformed by prior technological shifts, each of which changed the locus of religious power and authority. And while the players had often been different, arguably access to the means of disseminating information always depended on the combination of wealth and power and even class. Unpredictably, the current era of change has created an environment in which access to information, and the means of providing information, has fallen into the hands of the masses.

## THE DIGITAL REVOLUTION

The onset of the Computer Age emerged when telephony had been established as the primary means of interpersonal communication and the television served as the dominant modality for dissemination of information. Of course email and SMS texting soon replaced telephonic dialogue and then social media emerged as an even more powerful tool in this regard. Digital text, sound, and imagery can be copied, multiplied, and broadly disseminated at an increasingly rapid pace, and of course those materials are subject to the possibility of editing and revision as well. Even in the early decades of the digital age, the radically innovative World Wide Web, with the limitless possibilities for authorship and distribution, has been enhanced by the Web 2.0 technologies which have transformed the process of web-surfing from the one-way image of "downloading" to the interactive modality of a platform for both upload and download. YouTube, for example, (now owned by Google) is not merely a repository of endless volumes of video materials; it is also a broadcast mechanism for the individual creator to reach a potential audience of viewers and colleagues. And other technology giants such as Facebook and Apple have their own analogous platforms. These changes in communication modalities not only impact how succeeding generations will converse with one another, they also change the relationships between individuals, communities, information, and authority.

Even in the earlier stages of the digitization some media observers were already employing comparison to the revolution spawned by Gutenberg, as a 1998 Rand Corp. report noted, "The 21st century communications revolution may turn out to be every bit as dramatic, and entail similarly revolutionary and contradictory consequences, as the 15th century revolution. Some of these consequences may be just as beneficial, just as unintended, and just as socially damaging. Most will be upon us before they are socially appreciated." (Dewar, James A., "The Information Age and the Printing Press: Looking Backward to See Ahead," 1998 Palo Alto, CA: Rand Corp., 1998)

Looking for example at the realm of organized religion (and Jewish life is certainly not limited to only that area) the mode of communication and access to information traditionally reflected a broadcast model. Originally the dissemination of information and guidance was mediated by the oral tradition. The advent of written and then printed matter enhanced broadcast capacity as did electronic media. The digital communication model of the 21st century, however, radically alters the dynamic, not merely as a function of instantaneous technology, but because of the interactive nature of that modality. (See figure below.)

The membership of any given model exponentially increases the possibilities for interactive communication. Inherent in this process is a challenge to the conventionally hierarchical structure of many organizations, and religious communities that cannot remain immune to that mode.

Counter-intuitively, the advent of more advanced communications technologies can be seen as bringing society back to a scenario of more equal access to information and thereby more equal opportunity to gain power and exercise authority. Recognizing the reality that maintaining the infrastructure for our digital environment requires highly advanced skills and demands significant economic investment, nevertheless the basic literacy of online engagement is almost universal at this point, especially as mobile devices proliferate in the underdeveloped world. So as far as the user experience is concerned, we have effectively leveled the playing field to allow anyone to participate.

At the same time one can easily argue that the ubiquity of access and digital engagement has neither been accompanied or followed by an effective period of preparation and acculturation, as the changes come so fast and furiously that both individuals and communities have almost no time to adjust and develop behavioral norms before the next change is upon us. In accordance with Moore's law, in fact, each generation of technological advancement comes more rapidly than those which preceded it. This pace of change begs the question of whether we can ever catch up: Will the digital landscape "plateau" in some respect to establish a normative baseline to

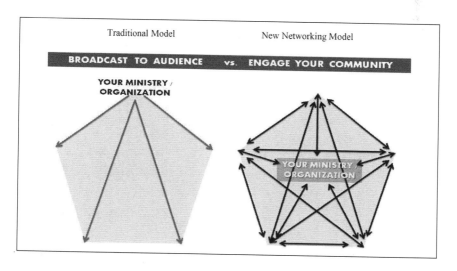

which society can respond - as ultimately occurred with the print revolution, and the development of early electronic communication? Alternatively, can the "industry," that creates and profits from the cyberworld they maintain be entrusted with the responsibility for encouraging or even enforcing codes of online behavior, and do we as citizens of both specific countries and the online universe want anyone at all exercising that sort of control?

A critical element of the challenge we currently confront with rapidly changing technologies reflects only the most recent iteration of the classic tension of modern religious life: how to preserve a consensus-based authentic Judaism while allowing Jewish individuals and communities to navigate the attractions and challenges of a more welcoming society (a tension some scholars would argue we see even as far back as ancient Judaism). Today's (and tomorrow's) digital landscape clearly heightens this dilemma. At what point do the innovative and individualized creative forces empowered by the internet's unfettered access challenge the authority and authenticity of tradition and indeed threaten the communal integrity and even solidarity that once united Jews throughout the world? We may take solace in the fact that communal leaders have been posing these very same questions throughout Jewish history, whenever potential ruptures to communal solidarity arose. And while the processes have not always been entirely peaceful and amicable, the Jewish people have until now survived those threats. As the digital revolution has not yet fully run its course, we cannot yet know how the Jewish people as such will emerge from the current challenge to solidarity, but if past is prologue there is good reason to be optimistic.

## COMMENTARY

*From Rabbi David Teutsch*: The world continues to change ever more quickly. The complex interaction among technological, evolving social factors, political shifts and economics is causing exponential increases in our world. Of course Jewish life must evolve to keep up. It is unrealistic to expect a broad-based consensus at a time of such turmoil. It is natural that the rate of Jewish experimentation is increasing and that subgroups become more disparate in their practice and in their views. We can bemoan this reality, but no effort to escape rapid change will be successful. The Jewish community needs to support experimentation and diversity as never before if Judaism is to thrive in the present era.

*From Rabbi Mira Wasserman*: Even as technological advances continue to serve as an engine for cultural change, old technologies persist alongside new ones in Jewish life. Thus, oral tradition remains central in Jewish life, in the practice of reading, teaching, and preaching from the Torah in synagogue. Centuries after the adoption of the codex, or bound book, we continue to read from scrolls in our rituals. And even as the study of the Jewish textual tradition has been transformed by digitization, many of us continue to cherish the distinctive tactile experience of pulling a volume from a shelf, of turning pages, of touching ink.

*From Imam Sami Aziz*: The Quran was given orally and through written form transmitted from the Prophet Muhammad pbuh to his companions. The entire empire received the same Quran through his close companion Uthman. Both Shia and Sunni use the same Quran. Oral transmission however is still extremely important with millions memorizing the Quran yearly. Every Muslim child learns by memory 5-10 small chapters of the Quran in Classical Arabic. It is stated by the Prophet Muhammad pbuh to be a merits and healing to memorize and/or recite the Quran for lay or clergy.

Dear Evolving Self (Dear Jeffrey, Dear Commentator),

*Chapter Seven*

# The Micro and the Macro: Responding to Dr. Amkraut's Portrait of Judaism and Technology

**SELF-AWARENESS,** balance, perspective

In response to Dr. Amkraut's panoramic sweep of Judaism and Technology, I often challenge both teens and adults to create 4,000 year-timelines that include 25 technological revolutions occasioned by particular inventions. Participants are then asked to speculate as to which of these 25 revolutions have had the greatest impacts on their personal, familial, and Jewish communal lives.

This activity often generates a great deal of storytelling about the "first time" a participant first encountered a new technology. Rereading Dr. Amkraut's chapter impresses upon me that the big map is full of many personal back stories. I am also struck by how the quickening pace of innovation as we enter modernity and post-modernity tests our basic dispositions towards change, tradition, and innovation. Below are two tales of mindset and technology:

1. Attitudes and dispositions towards technology and modernity from *The Education of Henry Adams*
2. The Digital Divide in the twenty-first century

## THE *EDUCATION OF HENRY ADAMS*

In chapter seven, of the *Education of Henry Adams,* "The Virgin and the Dynamo" Adams famously describes his encounter with the monstrous Corliss Steam Engine at the 1900 World's Fair in Paris. Our own response to his reaction is of course colored by the interpretive lenses of later generations. This provides a kind of Rorschach test for our attitudes towards technology and modernity as expressed in the accounts of John Freeman and Jonathan Rosen. We examine here both their eisegesis, the attitudes they bring to their own interpretation, and their exegesis, what they draw out of the encounter in terms of larger issues of our attitudes towards technology.

John Freeman, author of *The Tyranny of Email,* is certain that Adams sensed in the dynamo an absolute break with all his most closely held values of religion and beauty. After all, Adam enters the World's Fair just having completed his research on the cathedrals of Chartres, which captured the medieval synthesis of religion and beauty, rationality and faith. The dynamo threatened to ruin these delicate syntheses.

Jonathan Rosen, the author of *The Talmud and the Internet*, reads Adams encounter differently. It is not that Adams absolutely rejects the world of technology. At one point Adams almost begins to "worship" a certain God-like aspect of the machine. Standing in the massive "Gallery of Machines" Adams describes what amounts to a religious conversion. He begins to feel the forty foot dynamo as a moral force, much as the early Christians felt the cross.

*The planet itself seemed less impressive, in its old fashioned deliberate or daily revolution than this huge wheel, revolving at arm's length with vertiginous speed and barely murmuring—scarcely humming an audible warning to stand a hair's breadth further for respect of power—while it would not wake the baby lying close to its frame. Before the end, one began to pray to it, inherited instinct taught the natural expression of man before silent and infinite force.*

As part of the continuing education of Henry Adams, Rosen proposes taking him to a Jewish school (anathema to Adams who by many accounts disliked Jews). What he might learn there are the deepest lessons of adaptability and portability of the Jewish experience. Technology is simply one of the many challenges thrown at the feet of the Jewish people over time.

The enduring lesson here is that we live our lives within a complex amalgam of cultural assumptions, historical context, and personal, dispositional tendencies. Part of the adventure for the contemporary participant in digital life is to figure out in what ways she embraces and in what ways she resists changes in her own life that are dramatized but not limited to the digital arena.

# THE DIGITAL DIVIDE: NATIVES AND IMMIGRANTS

There is much discussion today about gaps between generations stemming from different relationships to technology. The most widely known is the so called digital divide that separates digital natives born after and digital immigrants born before 1980. Of course, everyone knows a millenial or Generation Z individual who is terrified by new technologies (or chooses to abstain from them) and there are any number of people from the immigrant generation who are quite savvy and agile in their uses of technology. As with all broad stroke characterizations, nuanced differences are sometimes missed.

A few analysts of the divide between natives and immigrants prefer softer, arguably kinder language. We are either digital residents or digital guests. In the analysis that follows below I explain why I prefer the edgier characterization of native and immigrant.

Digital life is itself characterized by language, or perhaps more precisely a series of dialects. Languages are quite often a signpost of tensions between the generations. The surface tension around language often masks deeper and larger issues of purpose and meaning and our assigned places within society. This becomes amply clear, in looking at selected letters from the 1933 Bintel Brief of the Yiddish newspaper, The Daily Forward (Metzker, 2001, 158). Like the columns of Dear Abby and Ann Landers which are arguably outgrowths of Bintel Brief dialogues, the reader is seeking advice from the "worthy editor" about parents who publicly insist on speaking Yiddish in public on the streets of New York City in 1933.

The response is a rather feeble, Fiddler-like nod to both sides. It would be nice if the children were less judgmental about their parents use of Yiddish. And of course, on the other hand, the parents should be more understanding of why their children find the public use of Yiddish so problematic.

It does not take a brilliant social scientist or historian expert in patterns of immigration to see that language stands here for assimilation into to the new host society. Typically, I will ask teens and adults reading the Bintel Brief selection to role play the part of the "worthy editor" and provide some wisdom to the five brothers.

I then will ask tongue in cheek whether there are "language" issues between the generations in their own home, knowing full well that English is generally the only spoken language in their home. My students are initially puzzled by the question. They remain perplexed until I unpack with them some of the insights of Marc Prensky, the educator who coined the terms "digital immigrant" and "digital native" (Prensky, 2001) (COM)

What shall we call these "new" students of today? Some refer to them as N for net-gen or D for digital gen. But the most useful designation I have found for them is Digital Native. Our students today are all "native speakers" of the digital language of computers, video games, and the internet.

So what does that make of the rest us? Those of us who were not born into the digital world but have, at some point in our lives, become fascinated by and adopted many ormost aspects of the new technology are, and always will be digital immigrants in comparison.

> The importance of the distinction is this: As digital immigrants learn—like all immigrants, some better than others—to adapt to their environment, they always retain to some degree their "accent," that is, their foot in the past. The "digital immigrant accent"can be seen in such things as turning to the Internet for information second rather than first, or in reading the manual for a program rather than assuming the program itself will guide us. Today's older folk were "socialized" differently from their children, and we are now in the process of learning a new language. And a language learned later in life, scientists, tell us, goes into a different part of the brain.

With the benefit of these insights my teen learners are more attuned to generational differences regarding attitudes towards technology. So, I then invite them to respond to a contemporary Bintel Brief:

Dear Worthy Editor,

I have this problem with my children. They are all pretty sophisticated in terms of their use of computers, technology, and the internet. My wife and I use computers and even the internet for our work as professors but we feel very "klutzy" with things like, Twitter, Facebook, Instagram and text messaging....

Our children show little or no compassion about this. They make my wife and I feel stupid.

Let me give just one example. I now text a couple of time a week. What was hardest for me to learn was how to place numbers and punctuation marks in my texts. The letters were much easier. Admittedly it must look to them like I am a seven year old based on the writing skills I do or do not demonstrate in my texts.

I ask you worthy editor. We have taught our children many things including being open to new ways of learning as they constantly do as they use technology. Is it too much to ask them to teach a few things about texting to us and to show a little compassion about our slow learning curve?

Sincerely,
A "Baby-Boomer" Parent

Dear Baby Boomer Parent,

Learn some things they don't know. Show them up. Do something digitally better than they do.

Sincerely,
Worthy Editor

Dear Baby Boomer Parent,

Not being a "digital immigrant" like yourself, I am only sort of proud of your accomplishments. It is good that you have learned how to text, but in these modern days, you need to know how to use all digital devices. Perhaps you and your wife could ask your "digital native" children to teach you how to use certain new programs. I'm sure that will help you explain to them that technology didn't develop this much until after they were born.

Sincerely,
Worthy Editor

For Prensky the gap is related to how our brains have been differently shaped by digital and pre-digital technologies. He suggests that the purpose of education for many centuries has been to deliver people from "darkness to light." While a noble goal, it is totally out of line with the reality that children today bask in light (here a metaphor for information). Beyond the funny stories of living on one side or another of the divide, there are serious issues that need to be considered.

"Whenever I go to school," says one student I know, "I have to power down." He's not just talking about his devices—he's talking about his brain. It's their after-school education, not their school education, that's preparing our kids for their twenty-first century lives—and they know it.

In chapter thirteen on the digital life of congregations we explore this same issue in greater depth and from the different angle of the "dark side" of the gap between digital natives and immigrants.

## COMMENTARY

*From Amelia Gavurin*: I agree that one is either a digital native or a digital immigrant. I think the language is a barrier not just between generations, but between colleagues at work. It can feel as though I am not just an employee that works on online engagement but also a translator to my digital immigrant co-workers. It is an unofficial, unspoken, and often unrewarded position of most millenial/gen z employees in this mixed generation work environment. While a real translator is seen as useful and learned, younger generations that offer digital translations are often brushed off in a rather condescending way by digital immigrants. While a yiddish speaking immigrant may value their translator, the same cannot necessarily said of the digital counterparts. This is unfortunate because language we speak is the language of the now and the future and should be valued as such by older generations.

Dear Evolving Self (Dear Jeffrey, Dear Commentator),

## Chapter Eight

# Judaism, Technology, and the Art of Living in Multiple Civilizations

**PERSPECTIVE,** balance, self-awareness

No concept is more integrally tied to the exploration of Judaism and technology found in this volume than the idea that Jews live in two civilizations, one Jewish, the other American. Positing a third civilization that is global and digital makes the equation even more complex. This notion was most fully explicated as a concept by Mordecai Kaplan in his 1934 *Judaism as a Civilization* (Kaplan, 1934, Introduction) One of the most elegant descriptions of the art of living in two civilizations civilizations comes from Milton Steinberg, a student of Kaplan, in his 1941 *A Partisan Guide to the Jewish Problem:*

If I may judge from my own life—and that of many Jews who share my viewpoint—the enterprise is amazingly undifficult. Let it be recalled that I acknowledge only one political political allegiance—to America; just I profess only one religion—the Jewish. Here there is no cause for conflict. Beyond that I have two heritages—the American and the Hebraic. English is my language and that of my children. I was educated in the public schools of my community. The history of America is my history. But Hebrew is my tongue too, and Jewish history my background also. Lincoln and Jefferson are my heroes together with Moses, Akiva and Maimonides. They all get along in my imagination most companionably. When I read Van Wyck Brooks on New England and its flowering and autumn it is of my own literary past that I am being instructed. I have studied Spiegel's Hebrew Reborn with the same sense of of identification. I sing Negro spirituals, American ballads and Hasidic or Palestinian folk songs with equal ardor. On the Fourth of July I set off fireworks and attempt to transmit to my children an appreciation of the significance of the occasion. With equal earnestness I kindle Hanukkah lights and discuss with them the meaning of that festival. At no time am I conscious of strain between the two worlds. I move from one to the other with such mindfulness that I am scarcely aware of the change of spiritual locale.

The first thing to note in thinking about what it means to live in two civilizations in 2018 is the replacement of binary forms of identity by multiplicity. Judith Plaskow had already noted in 1987 in *Standing Again at Sinai* that the hallmark feature of post-modernity is membership in multiple groups. In the digital age one switches spiritual locale even more rapidly and freely. Indeed, being part of the kind of global village envisioned by Marshall McLuhan already challenges Jews to live in at least three civilizations, without taking into account the very real differences between the spiritual landscapes of different local communities in North America and Israel (McCluhan, 1967, 63). (COM)

One also notes that it is an "idealized" vision. Many a Jewish educator has wrestled with the "s and s" dilemmas, tensions for families and congregations between commitment to soccer for their children and the simultaneous occurrence of Shabbat as a primary time for Jewish commitment. These educators understandably have a somewhat skeptical response to the suggestion by Steinberg that all aspects of the Jewish and American dance are "easy." Perhaps, at most, the relationship is an artfully improvised piece of jazz; it's hardly a beautifully choreographed classical ballet.

This then challenges Steinberg's notion of "compatible spiritual locales." Perhaps it is more honest and to the point in 2018 to talk about potential creative synergies and honest dissonances coming out of the very differences between the philosophical and relational worlds in which we live in as Jewish Americans. Here an insight from the work of the Jewish philosopher Emil Fackenheim is useful. Fackenheim expected that encounters between the different thought and valuational worlds of Judaism and the secular world would produce something that he called "mutually critical" insight (Fackenheim, 1973, Introduction).

Caplan and Schein speak to this point in a 2014 article in the *Journal of Jewish Education*:

> Fackenheim suggested that it is equally important for modern philosophy to be viewed from the perspective of Jewish thought as it is for Jewish thought to be viewed from the perspectiveof modern philosophy. Beyond the obvious corrective in the name of intellectual fairness (Judaism had most often sat at the throne of judgment of philosophers like Kant and Hegel), such an approach allows for a mutually critical encounter between any two substantive philosophies or methodologies of education where the virtues and blind-spots of each approach are highlighted by its encounter with the other.

This highlights a central dilemma of living digitally and Jewishly that I first drew out as a moment of pedagogic surprise in an article about Judaism and technology in the *Journal of Jewish Education* in 2015 (Schein, 2015) (COM)

I was preparing for Purim with my eighth graders. We had agreed that we would end our study with some good "edutainment," information that might add to the education of their peers and at the same time be very entertaining. A host of YouTube videos are viewed by the 8th graders and the prepared for class presentation.

One of my eighth graders asks for permission to share one more video clip. I grant the permission hanging on for dear life because even though my minimalist social media profile greatly increases the likelihood that everything posted is safe you never know what is out there.

So my student has uncovered from her Google search a Youtube video of my wife, my rabbi, and several close friends performing at a "goodbye to the Scheins" celebration in Cleveland with our Reconstructionist congregation Kol Halev dancing to the tune of the 1950s song "Come on Baby Do the Locomotion" with lyrics modified to "Come on Baby Do the Reconstructionist." I was thoroughly taken aback that the YouTube video has gone public (certainly not viral) and in the end delighted to have shared this with my students though it was not my choice. In fact, when a colleague has been speaking about a Jewish issue in classes and mentions the variety of Jewish orientations at the school and mentions Reconstructionism I see the lips moving and their bodies slightly swaying.

But in my dialogue with the students it becomes clear that their world of the Internet is completely open and has no attendant principles of ownership. To deploy a term of Jewish law everything is hefker, without any single owner, belonging to no one and everyone at the same time. Quite simply, if it is posted it is available for anyone's use.

Perhaps there is no conflict as fundamental in living as a Jew and living digitally as the tension between Judaism's absolute devotion to *beshem omro* (carefully attributing sources and cognitive ownership of ideas and concepts) and the often muddled mixing of points of view one finds on the internet. Elliot Dorff has usefully reframed these and other related tensions in a number of different contexts suggesting that we think of Jewish and American law/civilization as having overlapping, but differently weighted concerns (Dorff, 2007, chapter one). The weight of Jewish law is toward responsibilities, though it certainly has a language of rights as well. The weight of American law is conversely on rights, though every right arguably has correlative responsibilities.

The best way to capture and consciously utilize the powers of the overlaps, dissonances and creative synergies of living in these multiple civilizations where "text me" can mean ancient Jewish wisdom and also a form of social media and communication is to address them directly. Such ethical earnestness has precedence in Jewish tradition through the ongoing tradition of responsa literature where new realities were brought into dialogues with the wisdom of previous generations.

The traditional mode of *shaylah and teshuvah*/question and answer, is rooted in novel situations Jews faced that were either unanticipated or only partially described in Jewish law. Changes in context sometimes demand changes in content. Responsa literature has always been an engine of keeping Judaism fresh, alive, and relevant to the needs of the present moment. Responsa such as those that follow allowed Jews to keep their head in the heavens (connected to Jewish Law) and their feet on the ground (connected to the challenging complexities of new behavioral situations). They not only expect but honor and relish the situations that will create a moral or spiritual disequilibrium for the Jewish people. The provocations of everyday living expand the scope and creativity of Jewish tradition. (COM)

In what follows I attempt to model what a dialogue about specific digital dilemma might look like if it mirrored the dynamic interaction of Jewish wisdom and contemporary technology. It is part of a larger dream that I hope will become prominent on the *Text Me* website of a digital responsa center. Tellingly, one of the early responsa relates to what counts as privileged communication. In the tenth century Rabbenu Gershom issues a ruling that letters are a protected form of communication. No one may open a letter of another individual without express permission. New technology shifts our focus yet the ethical core of the dilemmas usually remain. It is not surprising then to find this mid-twentieth century responsum about the wide availability of telephone as a means of communication. Someone writes to Rabbi Jonathan Steif (Finkel, 1990, 167):

Question: Do you fulfill the mitzvah of *bikur cholim,* visiting the sick, by calling the patient on the telephone?

Response: There is no doubt that calling a sick person on the telephone is considered visiting him. Rambam classifies the mitzvah of visiting the sick under the heading of "loving your neighbor." This being the case, any favor you do for your friend, even if you do it by telephone is a manifestation of "loving your neighbor." Nevertheless, the essential mitzvah of visiting the sick should be done by personally going to see the patient. Seeing the patient's suffering will stir your feelings more than merely talking to him on the telephone will. It will cause you to pray more fervently for him and you will see more clearly what his needs are....

Fast forward eighty years and we live in an age of greater density of data and communication. What counts in 2018 as the most meaningful act of *bikur cholim?* Through email and texting we can almost instantly wish a person well. What do we make of this? Does the more frequent and numbers of good wishes in any way lessen their value? Would the "high bar" of a personal visit now be replaced by a "high bar" of a phone call? An email? A text? (COM)

Now in 2018 enter the world of love and romance. Whether embodied in Abraham searching for a wife for Isaac from his native Mesopotamia or Yenta looking to make matches in Anatevka in the movie *Fiddler on the Roof,* Jews are concerned with ethnic, religious, and cultural continuity. This search however has been transformed like everything else by new digital innovations. Now we can "swipe left" on the site Tinder. Swiping left is a way of instantly dismissing a person as a potential date/mate. So let us pose for Jewish investigation "Is it ethical to swipe left?" instantly dismissing a person based on a picture and the briefest of bios if the person is of no interest to us. By mutual consent of the people entering the site no explanation is needed for the rejection. (The newer "J-swipe" site softens the edges of the dilemma presented below but still I believe leaves us with a core ethical concern)

Prior to looking at the gesture through the lenses of Jewish law and values, it is useful to to imagine a spectrum of possible evaluative stances. The very positive (or at least benign) stance: This is nothing more than Yentl the matchmaker gone digital. People are always sorting and categorizing on the basis of physical attraction. This stripped-down version of other dating websites (like jdate) simply declutterers the fact that physical attraction motivates our dating behavior. As one millennial shared with me in an interview, "it cuts out the bullshit." Particularly in an age of stress and extraordinary multitasking we should appreciate the efficiency of Tinder. There is also a recognition here of the ultimate subjectivity of the digital matchmaker. A Hebrew saying asserts on matters of taste and smell that there is no rational argument. It is all a matter of preference. (COM)

On the other end of the spectrum is a very negative evaluation. The very act of "swiping left" involves the rejection of individuals based on the most superficial characteristics. This of course raises the question of whether it matters if the person being rejected never knows of the rejection. It also raises the specter of a digital meat market where the grossest forms of evaluation are used to judge individuals.

If we take as a given the Jewish values of *betzelem elohim*/people made in God's image and *kvod habriyot/*the dignity of each human being, does swiping left undermine these values? What of the fine notion from *Pirkey Avot*/Ethics of the Fathers—a book of foundational wisdom of the Jewish people—don't look at the cover of a person or object but rather discern its contents or character.

Yet, a defender of Tinder might point out that it takes time and communication to get to the core character of a person. Further, not all relationships are of equal depth and intensity. Appearance and attraction may be a necessary first step. Friendships also have value in and of themselves without the friend becoming *bashert*/one's life partner. And lest we be accused of an anachronistic puritanism let's remember that even if marriage is considered a societal prize for our relationship, commitment to life-partnerships is often delayed in our day. Yet, sexual need and expression are not. Tinder is also about "hooking up", finding satisfactory sexual partners.

Drawing from a different Jewish source, we might turn here to the work of the Jewish philosopher Martin Buber. Buber contrasts relationships that are deeply dialogical—I-Thou—with those that are instrumental—I-It. I-Thou relationships bring God and Godliness into our world of human relationships. I-It relationships "thingify" other individuals. Does swiping left lead to viewing the larger circles of people we never encounter (or here reject) as things? Buber actually finds it inevitable that we live a good deal of our life in the world of it, of things (Buber 2002, 54) Is this an acceptable example of one of those occasions? Further, do we want to draw a distinction between the phenomenon of swiping left—where ostensibly no one knows they have been discarded—and the emerging practice of "ghosting" where relationships of long standing are abruptly broken without explanation or dialogue?

So far we have been pursuing our analysis from the perspective of the "swipee" and what it might mean to be objectivized, even willingly. It is valuable to flip the perspective and ask what is the impact on the "swiper"- what is the potential effect on his or her character of swiping left? Here it is useful to return to our exploration in chapter four of the *middot* (character traits) of *musar* study and go a bit deeper.

One of these character traits is *savlanut*/patience (Morinis, 2007, 55)How does swiping left affect our capacity to wait for the best things in life to slowly ripen and come our way in good time? There is arguably an impetuousness to the act of "swiping left" that creates the wrong message for us about how we get the things in life we most value. Similarly *rachamim*/compassion, means forming slow and generous judgments about fellow human beings. What is the impact (conscious or unconscious) of herding so many people so quickly into a corral of the unacceptable?

Moral and spiritual dilemmas such as these will only continue to grow in the next decades. A digital space where ethically fraught issues can be weighed before being acted upon seems to be a very necessary concomitant of living in today's multiple civilizations.

## COMMENTARY

*From Dr. Brian Amkraut* On "Living in Two Civilizations In the early 21st Century." Arguably Jews, at least some of them, have experienced the dilemma of balancing multiple (more than two) civilizations for quite some time. As the consummate cosmopolitans in many of the major commercial centers from ancient times to the present, economically successful Jews had to strike that difficult balance of being at one and the same time locally minded (or even nationalist), Jewishly committed, and globally connected. Arguably Jews have been navigating the dilemma raised by the international global orientation of cyberspace for centuries. Of course Steinberg's commentary from 1941, along with Kaplan's original text, and I would throw in Louis Brandeis's famous quip equating Zionism with Americanism, dismiss the notion of dual loyalty all too simply by asserting unquestioned American patriotism alongside a commitment to Jewish peoplehood. The realization of modern Jewish political enterprise in a sovereign Israel does complicate matters. While in the early 1950s and even through the 1960s Jews could easily reconcile the compatibility of their support for Israel with their commitments to the United States, the reality of Israel-related politics in the 21st century makes this particular aspect of living in two civilizations slightly more complex than Kaplan initially laid out.

*From Rabbi Elliot Dorff:* "Question: Do you fulfill the mitzvah of *bikkur holim*, visiting the sick, by calling the patient on the telephone?" A parallel issue was addressed by Rabbi Avram Israel Reisner in a responsum for the Conservative Movement's Committee on Jewish Law and Standards, "Wired to the Kadosh Barukh Hu," available on the Rabbinical Assembly's website here: https://www.rabbinicalassembly.org/sites/default/files/assets/public/halakhah/teshuvot/19912000/reisner_internetminyan.pdf.

In it he asks whether you can be counted as part of a *minyan*, a prayer quorum, if you connect to the place where the service is being held through the internet. This is important for people who live in rural areas where a *minyan* may not be available and for shut-ins (that is, people whose health status does not enable them to leave home or the hospital), but it might also be convenient for people during the work week who want to participate in the daily afternoon prayer with a minyan but not leave their place of work to do so. Rabbi Reisner rules that a *minyan* may not be formed through the internet, that we need the presence of ten adult Jews in one room to do that, but if there is such a *minyan*, then others may log in and join them in prayer, including, for example, saying *kaddish* for a deceased member of the family on the anniversary of that person's death (*yahrzeit*).

*From Rabbi Steven Sager:* "Everyone who quotes a teaching in the name of its teacher brings redemption to the world." I might state it differently from the ancient (unattributed!) teaching in the Mishnah of Pirke Avot. "Redemption," after all, is an unwieldly term... Rather, I, say that attributing a teaching to its teacher fosters coherence... integrity, and honor for the history and the carriers of ideas (SS)

*From Rabbi Mira Wasserman:* It is time to re-imagine what Responsa literature looks like. Responsa literature presumes that there are legal experts who have all the answers, or at least have the requisite knowledge and authority to determine what answers look like. Inherent in Responsa literature is a hierarchy that privileges traditional forms of knowledge and authority. Today's technologies allow us to generate new forms of responsa that match our democratic values, and that recognize that younger people, especially those who are more at home with new technology, might have expertise that their teachers, parents, and rabbis lack. In my own work, I am experimenting with something I call "crowd-sourced responsa", looking to diverse sources of expertise for both questions and answers. In a newly-imagined Responsa, there might be multiple answers to a single question.

Dear Evolving Self (Dear Jeffrey, Dear Commentator),

*Part III*

# JEWISH LEARNING AND LIVING

*Chapter Nine*

# The Four Chasidic Pockets: Eighth Graders at Heilicher Minneapolis Jewish Day School Explore Judaism and Technology

**PERSPECTIVE,** balance, self-awareness

Over three years of teaching a course on Judaism and Technology for eighth graders at the Heilicher Day School in Minneapolis, I have tried to develop a substantive curriculum that balances expanding student awareness of the blessings of technology with the importance of applying Judaism's ethical and spiritual screens to guide our digital thinking and behaviors. The choice of eighth graders (typically thirteen and fourteen)) as the target audience for this work is intentional. They are steeped enough in digital worlds to understand their allure and potential, but still far enough away from total immersion to develop positions and perspectives as the next stage of their digital journey unfolds.

The balance in the curricular structures mirrors the four Hasidic notes discussed in chapter three. Sometimes I felt that my stance was too pro-technology; at others too anti.... Three years later I feel that I am embracing both sides of the dialectic in a balanced way.

So now I invite you into the world of *Text Me: Ancient Jewish Wisdom Meets Contemporary Technology* as if you were one of the eighth grade students at my first session where I present an overview of the whole course:

### THE 8TH GRADE HEILICHER COURSE ON JUDAISM AND TECHNOLOGY

Welcome. We will begin this trimester with a visit to the Pavek Museum of sound and digital technologies in St. Louis Park, Minnesota. While most specifically about the evolution of radio as a communications technology, we also will explore their television, computers, and other wireless technologies. You are going to love this visit! You will have an opportunity to create a radio broadcast focused on life here in Minneapolis. You will also become panelists in a quiz show testing the knowledge you've gleaned from our visit.

Right before leaving you will encounter the first of many debates you will experience during the semester. You will hear from one of your teachers—an enthusiastic, early adopter of all forms of technology—that you ought to trust almost any new technology to ultimately be good for you, the Jewish people, and the world. Then through the magic of a Jewish time machine Rabbi Israel Meir Kogan, the *Chafetz Chayim*/delighter in life), will regale you with a very harsh and loud blast of the Shofar to remind you that during these days preceding Rosh Hashanah and Yom Kippur the ability to say words and communicate so much doesn't mean that we ought to be engaged in such communication. The power of our tongues can clearly be used for good or evil.

Finally, a third teacher—less passionate and perhaps more clear eyed than the other two—will recommend to you the teaching of Maimonides about the importance of moderation in all things. He will counsel a middle way between the embrace and rejection of technology.

When we return we will practice a different way of gathering our wisdom. All through the course we will be utilizing an educational technology called Polleverywhere to crowdsource the wisdom of the whole class about the way technologies affect the kind of Jewish human beings we are and we are becoming.

When we return to our classroom studies you will be able to join a group of two or three other friends and begin studying the impact of technology on Jewish life and culture. Of course you will find a name for your team perhaps as odd as this past years: Cheese Graters, Calves of Steel, or Team #4 (of three). Eventually you will develop a team cheer as well.

With your teammates you will be challenged to put into chronological order the 25 technology revolutions, ranging from papyrus to smartphone, that transformed the world in ways large and small. You will be asked to make a case for which three technologies you think had the greatest impact on Jewish life. Then you will choose one technology that most interests your group and begin to learn a great deal about the history of that technology.

Before moving forward with presenting this technology to your fellow students you will need to consider two Jewish traditions. One is quite well known and the other not so well-known. The well-known one is reciting a blessing over the things in the world we appreciate, *hakarat hatov*/recognizing the good in the world. Below you will find a list of possible blessings that might capture your sense of appreciation:

Blessed is God who has inspired human beings to create so many interesting things in the world.

May God make sure that this new invention becomes popular and makes the inventor rich.

May the God who gives us wisdom make sure that this invention is used for good and not evil.

May God allow for this invention to be patented before all others.

May this invention renew all who use it. (COM)

Even though we know that blessings were not given at Sinai but created by *Chazal*/our wise Rabbis, there are some who make a case that one should not create a new blessing beyond what already appears in the Talmud and various codes. If this is your sensibility you will be exempted from this activity and return to your group when a new tradition, Special Purim, is explored.

It turns out that there is a tradition of communities declaring a "special Purim" (complete with a megillah scroll) when they have been delivered from extreme danger. There are several hundred such Special Purims recorded in the Encyclopaedia Judaica.

Your team challenge will be to connect the advent of a new technology with your choice of a special *brachah*/blessing and the declaration of a special Purim. You will need to develop a skit, song, or video that shows how your chosen technology once saved a segment of the Jewish people from great danger (or alternatively greatly enriched their lives). You will present these to other classmates and we will have a hadran/celebration with some modest party foods in celebration of your creativity.

So in some ways technology can be *kulo tov*/entirely good. But you are smart and ethically sensitive young adults, so I know you know that is not always the case. Technology can be used negatively as well as positively. We will begin to get ready for a unit on Awkward Family Photos called "To Post or Not to Post that is the Question." For each of five photos from the website you will have to make a decision whether it would be okay or not okay to post, if you were the central character in the position. Whatever your answer you will need to support your position with one of three critical Jewish values: yedidut/friendship, shemirat halashon/careful, ethical speech, betzelem elohim/the dignity of each individual as a creature made in God's image. In order to do this exercise well, we will explore in a philosophical way the nature of connections and what we mean when we say we are free or not free to do something. (TMW)

The next segment of the class is viewing five videos with your parents. These videos will repeat a message of the course that I trust is clear by now. Stretch and grow and find creative Jewish ways of using technology. At the same time several of them will emphasize how easy it is to allow technology to shape our habits rather than using it to become the kind of Jews and human beings we want to be. Your job will be recording at home both what you and your parents think and then bringing your ideas back to class for discussion.

Your final exam for the class is now on the horizon. We will sort through the various ideas we've developed about being a GJGDC ( a Good, Jewish, Global,Digital,Citizen). We will also study in some depth the *aseret hadibrot/* the Ten Commandments. Your final project will be to develop your own ten commandments for being a Good Jewish Global Digital Citizen. From this study the balance of positive and negative commandments and God and human-oriented commandments should become clear, so that your final project will also reflect that balance. (TMW)

You will be able to use anyone of a number of creative digital technologies to present your ten commandments. Knowing that you will be both thoughtful and creative, we will end with a second final hadran/, celebration of your Jewish learning. By then the phrase from the traditional *hadran* ceremony *hadran alan* (we will return to study) will be quite familiar to you. We will say hadran alan to one another as you leave, knowing that this process of becoming a GJGDC is a journey that we will each need to return to many times as the next several years of our lives unfold.

## THREE 2018 POSTSCRIPTS

Out of the learning of the spring semester of eighth graders at Heilicher emerge two important postscripts to this chapter. The first is the reflective voice of Noa Gross, whose eighth grade Capstone project was about teenagers and media. For the purposes of this volume it seems important to hear the concerns of teens in their own voice. Here Noa, a thoughtful young teen, provides more commentary on the Chasidic midrash of balance and two very different notes in one's pockets. Below is the beginning and end of her essay reproduced with both Noa and her parents' permission.

As an adolescent growing up in an increasingly technological world, I have witnessed the replacement of being present, with a screen. Although I am not against social media, with increasing rates of mental health issues (and social media more often than not a contributing factor), it is our priority as a society to look more deeply at something that has become an ingrained part of our everyday life. Social media is a complex subject with multiple factors that need to be both considered and understood The scales of pro and con (although not completely even) are fairly balanced, but what is being weighed is of great significance, and is not to be dismissed. Although social media is fairly new, multiple platforms have made a considerable impact on our everyday lisearch-ers are beginning to understand the underlying effects that social media has on an average adolescent. Social media, although a considerable technological advancement, has hastened the downhill projectile of adolescents body image, causing both long- and short-term health risks. As a society, it is the moral obligation of the people to come together, and ensure that enough counseling and education is readily available for adolescents, to guide them through this formative time in their lives ...

## Noa continues

Social media is both a technological wonder, and a growing threat to self-esteem and self-worth, and with the rapid expansion of new social media platforms, the world has not had a chance to catch up. Although we marvel at the amazing creations and communication on any type of social media platform, the question surrounding the harms attributed to the use of social media is concerning. The new generation must take charge and demand safer and positive social media sites, and in order to create this change real plans must be implemented as soon as possible. As a society, we must come together and demand more education for young adolescents exploring the new digital world.

Finally, I note an unanticipated unit that was not in the overview shared earlier in this chapter. The trimester corresponded with the political outrage related to issues of security and identity in regard to Facebook and the impact of providing Cambridge Analytica with information that may have played a critical role in undermining the fairness of the 2016 election process. I asked eighth graders if they wanted to join the fray and put Facebook on trial from the perspective of the three Jewish values (shmirat lashon/careful and ethical speech, hevrah/yedidut/friendship and community, and *kvod habriyot/ b'tzelem elohim*, the dignity of the human person that they had utilized as ethical filters in the To Post or Not to Post unit on Awkward Family Photos.

The eighth graders and I ultimately decided that it would be more interest-ing and productive to put Twitter on trial. This trial turned out to be a rich but very challenging process. Our director of technology and I opened a password protected Twitter account and allowed our eighth graders to follow a limited number of political and entertainment icons. Fortunately, the President of the Heilicher board was also a real life municipal court judge and agreed to preside over the trial.

One of the meta messages of the course was that as as a young adult one needs to be willing to understand diverse perspectives even when social media squeeze delicacy and nuance out of ideas by shouting views at one another. So it was important that the eighth graders be willing to take on either the defense or prosecuting attorney roles and to apply their best critical faculties as defense or prosecuting attorneys. After much dialogue two charges were filed against Twitter. They were: promoting divisive communication and reducing language to its most impulsive, least common denominator.

Midway through the trial preparations a crisis occurred. As a group we recognized that the deeply embedded ambiguity of whether we were putting Tweets, Tweeters, or Twitter as a social media platform on trial. This was no mere matter of semantic nuance. These were all interrelated of course, but,in the end, we decided it was the institution and platform that was being put on trial. In order to insure balanced judgment and perspective we concurrently engaged in nominating and awarding "Academy Awards" for best Tweets reflecting Jewish values from a list of Tweets from the Twitter accounts of our past four Presidents. The winner of that prize belonged to Barack Obama. The winner of the overall tweeting prize was Lin Manuel Miranda whose *Good Morning/Good Night* anthology of tweets is fast becoming a bestseller (Miranda, 2018).

Mixing metaphors of American and Jewish law, the judge collaborated with a *bet din/Jewish court of law* composed of three millennials, two of whom were graduates of Heilicher. Perhaps the deepest learning in the trial came when the judge invited the *beit din* to share its reasoning and any *machlokot leshem shamayim*/differences for the sake of heaven that emerged in their deliberations.

The puzzling and inconclusive ending of the trial (a split verdict on both counts) was Kafkaesque. We all left shaking our heads about whether we had conducted a fair trial or had just been lashing out at some of the more disturbing aspects of contemporary digital life. Perhaps we were also victims of the TMI (too much information) syndrome also part of contemporary digital life. We took in more information than we could really process.

Notwithstanding the experiment having gone somewhat awry, the eighth graders and I were able to end the semester with the Aramaic echo of hadran alan/ritually celebrating their commitment to treating these issues of communication and ethics seriously, as they moved on to high school.

As I play this curriculum forward I am aware in November of 2018 of a significant gap in its structure and hence a third postscript. Deeper attention to the "fake" in "fake news" is needed. A developmentally appropriate philosophical exploration of truth claims in media is very much needed in future iterations.

## COMMENTARY

*From Etan Weiss:* Heilicher is a pluralistic K-8 Jewish Day School with approximately 200 students in the 2017-2018 school year. The course I taught runs 3 days/week for 1 trimester. Each class session was approximately 45 minutes. The majority of these students own cell phones - though students are expected to leave them in their lockers during the school day. The school is a 1:1 school, providing each student with an iPad as a tool for their learning.

As mentioned earlier, the central messages and skills acquired during this course can always be taught using alternative foci and activities. What is important is student engagement and partnership that leads to personal relevance and lasting takeaways from the learning that set the stage for their Jewish adulthood trying to navigate technology as GJGDC steeped in Jewish values.

This is a crucial step to setting the stage and concretize technological developments as well as perhaps redefining technology for these students whose zeitgeist and worldview of technology is that it is all electronic!

"You will be asked to make a case for which three technologies you think had the greatest impact on Jewish life." One might suggest that we start with the impact on society or human development—but in the setting of a Jeiwsh Day School has the charge, both implicit and explicit, to show the convergence or at least lack of divergence of their Jewish identity from their human identity.

*From Peter Eckstein:* As I read these blessings questions arise. Who created them? Who are they meant for? Who are they thanking? The seem to be focused on a level of self interest that reflects a self serving attitude towards technology. Perhaps a blessing can be created such as: Praised be God for giving me the insight to explore my world in new ways and using new tools. Or perhaps: May The Source of Life grant that this new technology help those in need.

Dear Evolving Self (Dear Jeffrey, Dear Commentator),

*Chapter Ten*

# Towards a Brain-Friendly and Digitally Wise Model of Learning

**PERSPECTIVE,** self-awareness, balance

Paul Tillich once observed that the classical pedagogic error is "throwing answers like stones at people who have not yet asked the questions" (Houseley, 2006, 307-316). There is much in the tradition of Jewish learning that keeps us from committing this error. There are many Jewish texts underscoring the value of questioning as the root of learning. A core prayer of the daily, Shabbat and holiday prayer service *ahavah rabah*/great love underscores the multi-dimensionality of Jewish learning. The great gift of Jewish learning challenges us to *"discern, listen, treasure, affirm and act on"* our learning. (COM)

Further, many features of Jewish learning seem well aligned with both the digital revolution and the new discoveries made by neuroscience in the field of brain-friendly learning. Jonathan Rosen, the author of *The Talmud and the Internet*, was one of the first to find a counterpart to the "webbed" nature of digital learning in the cascading, non-linear progression of Talmudic thought (Rosen 2000, 10-11) he observed:

> When I look at a page of Talmud and see all those tucked intimately and intrusively on the the same page, like immigrant children sharing a single bed, I do think of the interrupting, jumbled culture of the Internet. For hundreds of years, Responsa, questions on virtually every aspect of Jewish life, winged back and forth between scattered Jews and various centers of Talmudic learning. The Internet is also a world of unbounded curiosity of argument and information, where everyone with a mind and modem can wander out of the wilderness for a while, ask a question and receive an answer. I take comfort in thinking that a modern technological advance mirrors an ancient form of discourse.

Arguments move rapidly across pages, often sparked by the repetition of the same phrase in a different context. The learning is associative and multi-directional. It is as if ancient hyperlinks exist that rapidly move our minds from one section of Talmud to another. What is going on beneath this learning that jumps from one topic to the next so quickly that one is tempted to call it stream of consciousness? The Jewish blessing embodying the commandment to learn points to the center that holds together the expanding associations. The blessing thanks God for *"la'asok bedivrey Torah"*/the opportunity to engage in learning. It assumes a web of ideas and associations will emerge from the process of engagement, perhaps not unlike the kind of webbing we call the internet. In the digital age, as in the Talmud, engagement and processing skills are thus necessarily and appropriately privileged over the pure learning of content. (COM)

The foundation of initial immersion and engagement is what is often missing from our Jewish educational environments today. Caine and Caine in their book *Natural Learning in a Connected World* (2011) reminds us how debilitating learning that is overly abstract can be. All learning moves along what they call a perceptual-action continuum. This substratum of the senses and perception is not only the best but arguably the only way rich learning can unfold. As the famous philosopher Kant once observed, precept and feeling must precede concept and reflection (Caine and Caine, 2011 49–78).

The best approach to educating in a way that aligns with the brain's natural inclinations is to pay attention to three sequenced phases of brain-friendly learning:

*Relaxed Alertness*
*Orchestrated Immersion in Complex Experience*
*Active Processing and Reflection*

Each of these phrases provides elegant midrash on the current emphasis on Jewish experiential learning. Relaxed alertness reminds us that educational experience cannot effectively occur in a neurological vacuum. Students can't and shouldn't simply be thrown into new experiences. A culture and atmosphere of trust and engaged exploration needs to be created in the classroom. Any hint of "fight or flight" will undermine the learning process.

The next phase—orchestrated immersion in complex experience—is demanding as well. Orchestration already hints that the role of the teacher has shifted from pedagogue to that of the organizer of educational experience, the guide on the side, rather than the sage on the stage. Immersion is also critical at this point. The material presented must be rich and deep, perhaps even a little mysterious. There is no direct transfer of knowledge along a narrow corridor of teaching as telling.

Yet as certainly as educational experience can't begin with abstraction, equally can it fruitfully end with pure experience without reflection. One can liken the process to a famous section of Mishnah (*bikkurim*) where the *peiroteihem,* the immediate fruits of the learning is the experience itself. Yet, the *keren kayemet*/enduring value of the experience, only emerges when dialogue, reflection, and and evaluation transform the experience.

This three tiered model is easy pedagogic advice to dispense to others. It is much harder to live out any pedagogic creed, as readers will see from the example below taken from one of my *Text Me: Ancient Jewish Wisdom Meets Contemporary Technology* family workshops:

> I have completed one of the signature activities of the Text Me family program, the creation of a chronology out of 25 revolutions in technology discussed in the previous chapter. Always there are discussions about the chronological placement of several innovations which are not as intuitively clear as parchment and Torah scrolls beginning the timeline and Skype and FaceTime completing it. I encourage people to use their smartphones to gather data about innovations that appear in relative proximity to one another, such as Pony Express and the Telegraph.
>
> One day an eighth grader has a gift for me. He has spent the whole two hours constructing a definitive timeline, gathered from his online research, while ignoring other tasks I asked of his group. He thought I might find it useful in the future. Self-directed learning utilizing technology had led to a better learning experience for him and a useful product for me.
>
> I am absolutely blown away. I remember the profoundly wise yet folksy advice from the Talmud, " Let your ear listen to what your mouth has said". I "know" that digital learning is reworking the wiring of our brains even as we speak. New models of learning are required to keep up with that and yet my workshops had a distinctly linear design.
>
> Similarly, I relearn the hard way that "talking" then "doing" is an invitation for pedagogic trouble with eighth graders. My classes are much more successful if the first thing they do when they come into class is respond to a question posed on the poll everywhere site. Then immersion precedes analysis in a way that is brain-friendly.

Several final considerations emerge from my teaching that are often noted in discussions in general education about digital citizenship. Again, a vignette from my work with eighth grades will highlight dimensions of how we access and utilize new knowledge.

It seems beyond argument that the web is an extraordinary knowledge resource. But of what kind of knowledge and how much? In my naivete I challenge my eighth graders to take the knowledge maps we had created of Purim and find three new pieces of information. "Where will we find it ?", ask the students. I respond instinctively, "Google it". Yes indeed, 7,900,000 entries as of mid-January 2016 likely approaching 8,000,000 now that several more Purim cycles have been completed.

Obviously I have given my students a sure prescription for entering *tohu vavohu*/the chaos of too much raw information. I try to regroup as best I can. We back track and have one of a number of conversations we had over the semester about trustworthy information. I try to narrow their frame by having them search three "trusted" websites (Chabad, My Jewish Learning, and Union for Reform Judaism) for information about Purim, also asking them to evaluate which site provides the best information for their work, and even to talk about the Jewish orientation of each site. Whatever pedagogic nimbleness I might be displaying at this point, however, I clearly created quite a mess by not more carefully framing the first steps of the inquiry. (COM)

Another perspective on dealing with a great deal of information comes when we turn to a selection from *Pirkey Avot*/foundational sayings of wisdom that deals with the *arba'ah midot*, the four kinds of learners who study with the wise. These learners are likened to the sponge, the funnel, the strainer and the sieve. Each of them processes knowledge differently. The sponge absorbs everything. The funnel retains nothing. The strainer collects all the wrong knowledge. (COM)

The sieve, which separates gross flour from fine flour, is the apparent winner of this staged knowledge contest. Instinctively one appreciates in the digital age meta-strategies that help us weigh and manage so much information. Yet there are also reasons to view this instinct as problematic. The terms *solet* and *kemach* as descriptions of material going through the sieve may betray archaic nutritional theory as well as what we have come to know about the brain's learning processes. *Solet* is the fine white flour separated from the *kemach,* coarser flour of the shell itself. Yet, nutritionally we have come to value the coarser flour because of the nutrients contained in the raw, unbleached product. Who, these days, touts the virtues of bleached white bread? In general while sieves and screens perform useful pedagogic functions they generally function best after students have grist for the mill, the raw chewy flour of complex knowledge(Bulka, 2008, 215) (COM)

## ADIN STEINSALTZ AND THE AMPHIBIOUS JEW

Here I would like to conclude with several insights drawn from the Talmudist-Kabbalist Adin Steinsaltz which highlights the potential for digital engagement to further both immersive, wholistic learning and more analytic learning in Jewish life.

Steinsaltz once observed in a lecture given in Jerusalem in 1993:

> All creatures live in water. The difference between sea creatures and land creatures is that land animals draw the water into themselves.

Undoubtedly, Rabbi Steinsaltz is aware as he writes this of a classical Jewish midrash told by Rabbi Akiva. The story begins with a conversation between a fish and a fox. The plot is clear. The fox would love for the fish to jump out of the pond and become the fox's supper. Why does the fish refuse? Like the Jew in relationship to the living waters of Torah, the fish cannot exist outside of the water.

Returning to Steinsaltz's epigram, there are two vital dimensions to all educational experience. One is marine. Engagement is the major trope of this work. It points to the importance of immersive venues where one can experience Judaism naturally and organically. It is aligned with much of what we have learned works in Jewish education in venues such as camp, Israel trips, retreats and some forms of early childhood education. Perhaps preeminently it permeates homes where the child's experience of Judaism begins at birth (or even in utero!).

The other mode is mammalian where Jews consciously journey to the house of their friends, their synagogues and communities to experience a very mindful Judaism that can guide them in creating spiritual connections as well as applying Jewish values to contemporary ethical dilemmas. Meaning making is its major trope.

These two modes may remind many readers of two important ideas in contemporary dialogues about experiential learning. The first is Mihály Csíkszentmihályi's notion of "flow"(https://positivepsychologyprogram.com/mihaly-csikszentmihalyi-father-of-flow). Initially, our richest educational experience has a marine-like quality of moving naturally through the medium that educates. When "rich complexity" is available and "well-orchestrated" the learner is so engaged with the learning that it is entirely focused and gripping. Perhaps it feels like one is a voice in the chorus of the song from the musical *Annie Get Your Gun,* "doing what comes naturally." Digital immersion may be our best tool for making sure that learning begins in the natural waters of free, exploratory learning.

Eventually these experiences need to be more fully orchestrated, perhaps borrowing more from the work of Lev Vygotsky the importance of scaffolds that invite exploration and stretch our minds. As Lisa Kolb reminds us in *Learning First, Technology Second*, it is the richer and more complex understanding of subject matter that matters most in our most sophisticated use of technology. The notion of scaffolds is the tool of choice for projects as we move from spontaneous to scientific concepts and create the cognitive and valuational structures that give substance and form to the educational flow initiated in a marine fashion. Wisely used, technology provides extraordinary tools for such extension and deepening of learning. (Kolb, 2017, 55-70) This mirrors Vygotsky's insights about the relationship between spontaneous and scientific concepts (Vygotsky, 1962, 106-110) While in theory it is possible to proceed top-down from the scientific to the spontaneous use of concepts, the process works best in the other direction, from bottom-up.

> In working its slow way upward, an everyday concept clears a path for the scientific concept and its downward development. It creates a series of structures necessary for the evolution of a concept's more primitive, elementary aspects, which give it body and vitality. Scientific concepts, in turn, supply structures for the upward development of the child's spontaneous concepts toward consciousness and deliberate use. (Vygotsky, 1986, p. 194)

## COMMENTARY

*From Etan Weiss:* The Passover Seder as the paramount American-Jewish family ritual wherein all of the intricacies at the heart of the seder is so that your children will ask a question

*From Rabbi Steven Sager:* An ancient sage taught: "A weaver proceeds with confidence when certain that the warp of the loom will hold... We are the web and You [God] are the weaver." *Being* the web—the weave of our ideas and associations—in the best possible way is our daily responsibility. The Aramaic, masechet, meaning both "web" and "loom," is the term for a tractate of Talmud. Each masechet/web of Talmud, explores a unique topic such as Shabbat, Contracts, Purities, and Blessings. Each masechet is a "life-loom" into which we weave living experience.

*From Peter Eckstein:* What is *solet* and what is *kemach*? What has value today vs. value yesterday? In Jewish life and learning, the answers change. Our understandings reflect current reality. So, yesterday's *solet* may be today's *kemach.*

*From Dr. Mary Hess:* I am reminded here of the comment John Seeley Brown and Douglas Thomas made in their book "a New Culture of Learning"

(Create Space, 2011) where, in commenting on the challenges of the web, they wrote:

The new culture of learning is not about unchecked access to information and unbridled passion, however. Left to their own devices, there is no telling what students will do. If you give them a resource like the Internet and ask them to follow their passion, they will probably meander around first feel heard before they are willing to listen. All the facts in the world are not compelling. It is the process of feeling heard that makes space for learning.

Many of us in Christian settings have found ourselves drawing on the Greek concepts which were foundational to many of the Second Testament texts—techne (to do, craft or art), nous (understanding, thinking about thinking), phronesis (practical knowing, practical wisdom), sophia (knowing love, mystical wisdom), episteme (to know how, scientific knowledge). Far too many of our current contexts artificially separate out these forms of knowing, keeping them apart from each other, trivializing some and emphasizing others. Digital media offer us an environment, an ecology, within which we can bring these perspectives back into a rich and holistic space of integration, finding bits and pieces of information that move them from topic to topic—and produce a very haphazard result.

Instead, the new culture of learning is about the kind of tension that develops when students with an interest or passion they want to explore are faced with a set of constraints that allow them to act only within given boundaries." (p. 81)

I would note, however, that it is also worth recognizing how rich an experience comes from being willing to "not know." And then demonstrating, alongside of students, what it means to search for information in the vast sea of the net. There is a very famous Christian text, in one of Paul's letter to the community gathered at Corinth, where he writes that he comes to the community "...proclaiming the mystery of God, I did not come with sublimity of words or of wisdom. For I resolved to know nothing while I was with you except Jesus Christ, and him crucified." (1 Cor 2:1) Although some Christians have distorted Paul's words, many of us hear that text as an invitation to deep humility, and using love as the source of all knowing.

Dear Evolving Self (Dear Jeffrey, Dear Commentator),

*Chapter Eleven*

# Jewish and Human Identity: Erik Erikson, God, and the Divine Image in the Digital Age

*SELF-AWARENESS,* balance, perspective

We had just finished one of the signature family programs developed as part of the *Text Me* project. This was a decision-making unit based on photos drawn from the website Awkward Family Photos (https://awkwardfamily photos.com/) The activity's goal was to put oneself in something of a Raw-lsian "original position." Would I be comfortable if this photo—sometimes humorous, sometimes embarrassing—were posted and I was the primary character in it?

The debriefing involved a dialogue about who will see these posts. The answers are usually quite predictable and conventional: anyone who cares to look... whoever knows you might have posted... anyone who has access to the web...etc. The "being brought up short moment" came with the response of one 8th grader, perhaps half serious and half tongue in cheek: God is watching!

The silence of the group spoke volumes. Much has been written about our character being on the line when we go online. This response pointed to a whole arena missing from our collective dialogue about digital life. *Hashga-cha pratit/*divine providence is God's watch over God's creatures. Organizations like Common Sense Media (https://www.commonsensemedia.org/) are appropriately focused on the human dimension of our digital relationships (*bein adam le'chaveiro),* with a particular emphasis on raising good digital citizens and healthy children in a connected world. Yet, what of the character-building and "religious" side of posting and creating our social profiles? The question of how we deal with the intersection of the divine and human dimensions of life is worthy of further exploration. We begin by starting with the human side.

The multiplicity of possible selves available for creation and re-creation via social media poses significant questions about my "real self." Teens in various focus groups I have run sometimes downplay and sometimes are genuinely bothered by the possibility of losing one's true identity. Turkle (2011), also has reservations about whether the manicured images of self that one can develop and project on social media are manifestations of teens' and adults' real selves. The human and religious core of the self are thrown into new light by the challenges of the world of web 2.0 and 3.0. The ancient understanding of human beings as having been created *betzelem elohim*/in God's image is problematized in interesting ways when multiple pathways for expressing and creating the self emerge. As Turkle observes about Second Life, a platform popular from 2003–2010 that plays a quieter but still significant role in our media landscape:

> Technology proposes itself as the architect of our intimacies. These it suggests are the substitutions that put the real on the run. The advertising for Second Life, a virtual world where you get to build an avatar is quite clear: "Finally a place to love your body, love your friends and love your life." On Second Life, a lot of people, as represented by their avatars, are richer than they are in first life and a lot younger, thinner, and better dressed(Turkle, 2012 *Alone Together* Ted Talk)

## GOING DEEPER: BETWEEN IDENTITIES HUMAN AND DIVINE

We all care about nurturing strong, healthy, dynamic, human and Jewish identities. We are also, theologically speaking, concerned with our belief and experience of being created *betzelem elohim*/in God's image. I believe in both these things but in all honesty I have more questions than answers about their interrelationship.

When we place our religious traditions in historical context, we recognize the complexity of our most precious ideas—the fact that they too have an ideational back story. So the very concept of *betzelem elohim* means different things to different Jewish thinkers. For Maimonides it is clearly anchored in the intellect. For Ramban it refers to our soul. For Rabbi Meir Simcha Cohen of Dvinsk it is our free-will. For Martin Buber it is a process of self-actualization, perfecting the capacities within us in a divine way (Olitsky, 2016)

All of these conceptualizations, different as they might be in their theological wrappings, are linked at their valuational core to another Jewish concept, *kvod habriyot*/the dignity of the human person. Precisely because human beings are made by God and in God's image they are of inestimable worth. In the political life of the American people we make our "rights" inalienable. In the western monotheistic traditions it is the "worth" and "dignity" of the individual that is inalienable.

How does this square with the understandings of human identity, growth and development nurtured by the social sciences? Consider for a moment the gifts of understanding bequeathed to us by Erik Erikson. Referred to by his biographer Lawrence Friedman as "identity's architect", Erikson's seminal contribution to think of identity as spreading across an entire life cycle (not being set by age five as with Freud) and in constant flux. Friedman notes that Erikson was a master of boundary crossing. At once and at different times he was Danish and American, Jew and gentile, psychoanalyst and anthropologist, activist and scholar. All these polarities were held together by a delicate tissue of what Erikson called the "self," the feeling of continuity amid all these variations. Some of Erikson's disciples writing between 1970 and 1990 began to worry that this sense of "self" suffers from "identity vertigo," too many experiments with our identity (Friedman, 1999, 478)

Especially in the digital age we need to raise questions of what it means to fully embrace the idea of identity plasticity. We return to Sherry Turkle's comments earlier in the chapter about the opportunities for new identities promoted by Second Life. I once went through this process of developing my own SL avatar-based identity so I could understand the dynamics of identity formation from a teen perspective. I chose to make my avatar Janusz Korczak the influential Polish Jewish educator best known for his march to death with children during the Holocaust, but the site itself was disappointing as someone else had already taken that identity and the site gave me a different one.(COM)

Clearly, there are multiple ways to understand this process of identity experimentation. It means, for instance, something very different to imagine it as identity *enhancement, rather* than identity *displacement* or *replacement.* Our most evolved contemporary understanding appreciates the notion of *bricolage,* the formation of complex identities as a process of exploring pieces of forgotten or undeveloped aspects of self that constitute personal wholeness. Inevitably, our own subjectivity will put a positive or negative valence on the speed and direction of identity experimentation.

Theories of *mimetics* value the self discovery that is part and parcel of our highly digital lives. We can see and imitate new identities while having them mirrored back to us and reinforced with blinding speed. Clearly, many teens and not a few adults develop a quantitative metric for their own self-image based on how often they have been liked and how people respond to their social media profile. One wonders what happens to the sturdy theological bulwark of thinking of one self in the image of god as this process unfolds There are easier answers to this question for others than there are for me. Rabbi Dr. Asher Meir, the "Jewish ethicist" was asked by a reader whether it is okay to have a fantasy identity. His responses set some fairly narrow parameters for identity formation. Using a metaphor from an earlier, non-digital time, he grants that of course teens should experiment in the sense it is healthy to give nuance and style to one's own handwriting and distinctive signature (Asher Meir, 2005, 215)

Beyond these parameters, however. one moves into potentially dangerous territory. Dr. Meir cautions teens about cross-dressing for instance because Jewish distinctiveness requires separate roles for men and women. He also worries that these new identities will displace rather than augment our sense of being made in God's image.

For most non-Orthodox Jews, including me, such a response is far too narrow and arguably even unethical. But having rejected his answers I am left with an uneasy sense that the excitement I experienced as a young Jew exploring the interface of the truths of social science about human identity and the truths of Jewish tradition has worn thin. Processes more complex and ambiguous are at work than my mortal mind can comprehend.

At this stage of my life I am perhaps more anchored by the insight of Emil Fackenheim (1974, *Encounters Between Judaism and Modern Jewish Philosophy,* chapter one) about encounters between Judaism and modern philosophy. These encounters, he argued, are at their best "mutually critical." One learns more of the rich competencies as well as the unattended shadows and blank spaces of each discipline through the encounter.

Within that mutually critical framework, I am glad that the wonderfully complex dynamics of identity formation keep challenging our more settled notion of being a Jewish human being. I am equally glad that the notion of being made in God's image keeps us from the idolatry of enshrining our own identity experiments.

## COMMENTARY

*From Peter Eckstein:* What is the relationship between identity plasticity, kvod habryot and B'tzelem elohim? If we shift who we are, does it make it easier to revise the absolute meanings of the Jewish/Hebrew concepts? Are they absolute or relative, depending on who I am at the moment? Second Life was like putting on a mask, allowing the user to reinvent them self. How does this impact the way we interact with the other? Perhaps the question is should it?

*From Dr. Adina Newberg:* The poet Rivka Miriam challenges us to remember how we all evolve into different selves and different identities as she describes the black hole that consumes all stars and is life itself. Referring to a group of delegates/scholars attempting to understand it she says:

*the hole is here and also there.*
*It's in the bottle and the stopper, alone and in a group.*
*It's in the list each delegate has written in his notebook*
*and is the delegation itself.* (AN)

Ali Mohar describes the what could be a counterintuitive moment of recognizing G-d in a mundane setting. He sees a beautiful tourist bathing in the Tel Aviv sun and says:

*It is true, I look at her for myself*
*But a little bit for you*
*Because I know you are inside me*
*The same way I am inside you.*
*And maybe I was created*
*So you could see from within me*
*The world that you created*
*With new eyes.*

*From Dr. Adina Newberg:* The confluence of technology and *betzelem elohim* comes forth in a challenging poem by Admiel Kosman, a poet, a Talmudist and professor of literature: Admiel Kosman writes both in Hebrew and in English. This particular poem is written in English: In the poem, the human communicates with the Divine one, but ironically he is the one "installing" him, like one installs a computer program. Is he creating the God he is talking to?

*Installing You my Lord, in da middle of the night.*
*Installing You and all Your programs. Up and down*
*da night goes, in my Windows, slows, installing You and*
*da kruvim, installing you and da srafim, installing all*
*da holy crew, until da morning*

*From Reverend Teri Elton:* Identity, of course, is not a binary construct. As both divine and human, a life of faith is a formational journey. If people of faith believe they are created in God's image and live in and amongst the world, identity is a both/and reality. God gifts identity, as it is also formed and shaped by engagement with society. Anchored in God and open to the world, it must remain dialogical. As long as God's part remains in the dialogue we have someplace to tether the formation process to. God is faithful.

*From Rabbi Hayim Herring:* Perhaps we are confusing two different issues: one, that all people are created in the Divine image, guaranteeing equal and inherent human dignity. That inherent dignity is a constant that does not vary by age, gender, religion, or ethnicity. But does being created in the Divine image imply that image is static? Indeed, it's clear throughout the Bible that God's image is "plastic." God appears in multiple forms as a parent (both mother and father), as a judge, as a compassionate being, as a "lover" of humanity at one time, and a destroyer at another. While remembering that being created in the Divine image means no one person is privileged over another, should we be so concerned about "bricolage" and "identity plasticity" when those concepts may also be related to being created in God's image (See for example Mekhilta d'Rabbi Yishmael 20:2)

*From Rabbi Elliot Dorff:* Contemporary video games use graphics that are much more realistic than those available ten or twenty years ago. As a result, users more easily identify with the characters in the game. Playing most video games is fun and sometimes even educational, as long as playing such games does not take over one's life. What about, though, the segment of video games that are violent or discriminatory—"Grand Theft Auto," for example. Is it good for you to imagine yourself killing people at random, with larger numbers of points for police officers or pregnant women? Rabbis Elliot Dorff and Joshua Hearshen wrote a responsum on exactly that question, "Violent and Defamatory Video Games," that can be accessed on the Rabbinical Assembly website: https://www.rabbinicalassembly.org/sites/default/files/assets/public/halakhah/teshuvot/20052010/videogames%20Dorff%20Hearshen%20Final.pdf

*From Amelia Gavurin:* I see identity experimentation in the digital age as more of a branding experiment. Teens and young adults want to cultivate what they believe is an aesthetic that represents them authentically, but from different viewpoints. On Facebook I can have a wholesome, family aesthetic, on Instagram a perfectly curated life, on Twitter a sassy wit. It is no different than being one way in religious school, another way in synagogue, and a third way at home with your family for Shabbat. Identity and the expression of it varies based on location and company and that can be seen on online platforms as well.

*From Dr. Mary Hess:* What Elizabeth Drescher, Keith Anderson, and many other commentators in the Christian space have begun to point out is that digital media—particularly social media—are based on algorithms that actually make it much harder to have these separate, isolating, different "selves." I would tell the story of a friend of mine, whose daughter desperately wanted a facebook account when she was 11 years old, because all of her friends were communicating that way. Her parents refused, telling her to wait until she was 13. She went ahead and set up an account anyway, thinking she could manage it with settings such that her parents would never know. The algorithms, however, defeated her, because one day quite apart from her intent, facebook asked her father to friend her, simply based on her other friends list. Even Sherry Turkle has begun to recognize that there are myriad ways to be "alone together" that draw on representations of what it is to be human that are more fluid, more relational, and more interconnected than we have been willing to acknowledge.

*From Dr. Mary Hess:* Here I think Robert Kegan's more contemporary take on developmental psychology is useful. He writes explicitly about the various challenges to our identity formation and psycho/social growth that are embedded in the rapidly changing contexts around us. We are in many ways "in over our heads" (the title of one of his books). But he also notes that it's ok to be "in over your head" as long as someone is reaching out a hand to help. The problem comes when you are drowning and there are no hands in sight.

*From Dr. Mary Hess:* Danah Boyd, a key commentator and social scientist who does empirical research with teens and digital media suggests "it's complicated" (the title of one of her books). She argues that the social network around teens needs to be made up of multiple partners. It might not be a parent who is "friended" with their daughter or son on Facebook, but rather an aunt or uncle, or a mentor from a congregation.

*From Dr. Mary Hess:* Michael Rosenak, a Jewish educational philosopher, describes a religious identity that is "loyal, but open." In Christian settings we have found it useful to use the notion of a "centered set" rather than a "bounded set" when talking about identity. That is, emphasizing core, centering assertions—we are made in the image of God, God takes on flesh to share God's love into the world in concrete terms, and so on—allowing the many other contested and diverse edges of Christian identity to be more porous (marriage issues, sexuality issues, and so on). A "centered set" identity rests in the center and is rooted enough to be flexible on its edges, whereas a "bounded set" identity has sharp edges and is defined by who is "in" and who is "out." Given our much more complex understanding of authority i in a digital world, we must remember that we have to build credibility for our ideas, and draw people into relational and accountable authority for our religious identity, rather than assuming or imposing it.

*From Dr. Brian Amkraut:* On "Betzelem Elohim" and the notion of God's creative force: Perhaps one aspect of identity fluidity, and specifically the creation of a new "image" on line is a very rejection of the divine role in creating mankind. Is an individual who prefers an alternative avatar that upends rather than truly reflects their IRL image and persona also fighting against the divine image in which they were created. Do they not have an opportunity on line to create *ex nihilo*, as it were, the true self that God denied them, challenging the divine order in a modern-day Tower of Babel?

Dear Evolving Self (Dear Jeffrey, Dear Commentator),

*Chapter Twelve*

# Communication and Community in the Digital Age

**BALANCE,** self-awareness, perspective

## COMMUNICATION

Given the very real forces of chaos and disorder in our lives, communication is a *nes gadol*/great miracle. We live in the constant shadow of the 11th chapter of the Hebrew Bible, the story of the Tower of Babel, where human effort is thwarted by impossible communication issues. The popular app for teaching foreign languages, *Babbel,* delights us with our capacity to playfully overcome the forces of linguistic and semiotic entropy by learning new languages, new systems of communicating meaning.

Our understanding of the great miracle of communication is also underscored in a blessing related to the revelation of the Torah at Mount Sinai. Famously, Jewish interpretive tradition posits that each of the 600,000 witnesses to the revelation of the Torah experienced this event in significantly different ways not intuitively clear to other human beings. Only God is to be praised as the One who understands the secrets of each person's mind. *(TMW)*

There are special dilemmas and paradoxes of communication in the digital age. The extraordinary ability to google and share information exists in tension with the potential for trivialization and abuse of information, heightened even further in the era of "Fake News." A quick look at both sides of the paradox is valuable.

Marc Prensky, the educator who coined the idea of "digital natives and digital immigrants" believes that for several millennia our whole educational enterprise was based on an understanding of teachers guiding students from darkness to light, from ignorance to understanding. Digital information is the game changer that overturns this paradigm since we live in an age where we all bask in the light of available information.

The other side of the paradox is brevity bordering on incoherence. Twitter's initial 120 (now 240) characters is the paradigmatic example of such contraction. Yet, such contraction is not always negative. The same letter "c" begins clear, compelling, and cogent. We do well to keep an open mind and not follow the example of the Missouri school teacher who published a letter in 1936 suggesting that Dizzy Dean, the famous pitcher turned colorful baseball announcer, was ruining the lives of school children by corrupting the proper speaking of the English language.

I would suggest that the real challenge of digital communication is captured by the metaphor of communication having an *accordion* like nature. Sometimes we need to compress language. At other times we need to employ an expansive mode of communication.

In regard to the compression mode of the challenge, the story of a non-Jew urging Hillel to summarize the whole Torah while standing on one foot receives mixed reviews from Jewish interpreters. Some sneer at the possibility of reducing a rich, complex, document like Torah to a more digestible chunk of information. Others join in the fray making their own suggestions of what the most brilliant contraction would look like. One midrash enjoins us to "say little and do much" while a different voice suggests that we ought to continuously enlarge upon and embroider the narrative of the exodus from Egypt at our Passover seders.

For Jonathan Rosen, author of *The Talmud and the Internet*, the accordion expands continuously. Rosen focuses on the cascading nature of Talmudic conversation and likens it to his experience of the emerging internet of the late 1990's. He concludes that communication is richest when it is guided by an unbounded curiosity and moving simultaneously in several different directions (see chapter 7 of this volume for additional insights from Rosen). (COM)

Inevitably communication returns to a compressive mode. Perhaps the best modern analogue to "the Torah on one foot" is the cottage industry of six word novels generated by Larry Smith's creative spin on the challenge to Ernest Hemingway to write a six word novel. Hemingway's novel "baby shoes, for sale, never worn" (is it apocryphal? ... both easier and harder to determine in the digital age) became the prototype for others striving to express something substantial in few words. An example of the use of this approach as an educational tool was shared in chapter three through the six word novels created by eighth graders to express their relationship to technology.

There are numerous ways to understand this communication paradox. Perhaps the simplest is to access the self-help language of Alcoholics Anonymous.

"God teach me to change the things I can; accept the things I can't change; and the wisdom to know the difference between the two."

Similarly, we can hope for the wisdom to know when brevity and when loquaciousness should be the primary virtue for our communication in a given context.(COM) Yet, the dilemmas of contemporary digital communication are arguably *sui generis.* In general, one can apply the wisdom of Aristotle or Maimonides in trying to find a golden mean when deciding to lengthen communication after taking a shortcut or expanding it when the result is too cryptic.

Yet the golden mean or comfortable middle has some strangely insidious different meaning in the digital age. Turkle writes of an interview with a young woman as she tries to document the "goldilocks syndrome": *Sarah describes herself as a modern day Goldilocks. Her texting and smartphone enable her to handle her relationships in a way that is "exactly in the middle." People are close enough to be constantly connected but distant enough so they can't make real demands on her. A phone conversation would disrupt this balance. (from TED talk, 2012)*

I will return to this notion of guarded communication that takes on the form of a quantitative metric, measured by how often one is liked or appreciated on Facebook and other digital platforms, in Chapter Fourteen in the form of a contemporary midrash on Soliveitchiks' Adam I and II first encountered by the reader in Chapter Five.


## COMMUNITY IN THE DIGITAL AGE

The questions of what and how we communicate are intimately related to that of *with whom* we are communicating. Here I begin with two personal notes. Though I have a facebook account as well as instagram and twitter accounts, I mostly access social media through my wife. I am, of course, delighted as I imagine most of my readers are, with a picture of a family member (particularly a grandchild!) beaming or doing something funny but I limit my participation.

On the other hand—again the stunningly recurring role of paradox in this Volume—I am a convert to the rich potential of virtual communities. As a professor of Jewish education, I have overcome my own inner mantra of "teaching online can't be as authentic as teaching in person." Between 2000 and 2012, I had the privilege of helping guide over one hundred students through their Masters in Jewish Education program at Siegal College in Cleveland. This could only have happened with the help of digital technology and would have been impossible had they had to journey to the Laura and

Alvin Siegal College of Jewish Studies. Students from communities as geographically diverse and far-flung as Atlanta, Milwaukee, Kansas City, Miami, Israel, and Vancouver, Canada could only visit my classroom in Cleveland virtually. (COM)

I also saw evidence of the different and more powerful *voices* developed *by* learners when they were freed from the constraints of traditional classrooms. By course design, everyone was required to participate, not only the most verbal as so often happens in real time classrooms. As a rabbi, I have also watched many adult Jewish learners gain voice and knowledge as they prepared a talk for synagogue, searching the internet at their own pace (and perhaps in their pajamas!) All of this does not take into account the power of digital community when the frail and sick can join the religious services of their community by clicking on a link. Further, once my Jewish concerns about *tikkun olam*/world improvement and transformation are taken into account, can I be anything but impressed by the account of David Kilpatrick in *The Facebook Effect* of how one of the first virtual communities was the over million people who joined a acebook group dedicated to overthrowing the repressive FARC regime in Columbia (Kilpatrick, 2010, 1-19)? I have often imagined (but failed to fully enact) the gift of digital immediacy leading to my transforming the older study tradition of doing a *daf yomi*/page of Talmud a day into a *mitzvah yomi*/a communication addressing some pressing issue of social justice each night before I retire. Professor Jeffrey Mahan's description of the *After Hours* program at the University of Colorado's Iliff School of Theology in Denver is a particularly well drawn portrait of the power of digital culture to engage in social activism (https://www.facebook.com/AfterHours-Denver-100700400022534/?fref=nf)

So if I grant *lehatchilah*/from the very beginning, that in the twenty-first century community takes on many creative and diverse forms, what is reasonable "mistrust" regarding the reshaped notions of community in the digital age? (COM)


## THE HUMAN FACE IN FACEBOOK


For Mark Zuckerberg, founder and CEO of Facebook, there is a triple value proposition to Facebook: transparency, unstinted sharing, and—perhaps most profoundly—the return from a capitalist money economy to a "gift" economy. Perhaps the greatest gift is that of the human face. A series of Facebook public relations commercials in 2017-2018 begins and ends with tender, beautiful, poignant and funny clips of human faces. In between the bookends of unquestionable meaning is the villain: The rapid fire deployment of stolen identity, fake news, and public shaming that deface Facebook. In the commercials Facebook promises to eradicate these as it makes the "radical" move of returning to its original mission.

Throughout this volume I have an explorer of my own quite unfinished evolution as a global digital citizen, in addition to being an academic, a spiritual coach and educator. Now, perhaps unsurprisingly, I do not provide answers, but share my own questions about community using five very different Jewish texts to explore the shadow side of Facebook. My concerns are more subtle than the flagrant abuses which so often draw our attention in exploring social media ethics. The same analysis would hold for other forms of social media such as Instagram or Twitter.

The first text comes from *Berachot,* a section of Talmud that deals primarily with the kinds of blessings we might offer. An amazing array of questions surround the imperative to both give thanks and acknowledge obligatory rituals. With whom should we say such blessings? What specific situations render the blessings unnecessary or even forbidden? What precise combination of Hebrew words give the blessing full force and power?

In one section some Rabbis pose the following question. It is known that the presence of at least three people is necessary to recite the *zimun*/introductory formula of *birkat hamazon*/the blessing after a meal. So what if, the Talmud conjectures, one of those three goes off to the market. Can the remaining two still say the blessing?

Well, it turns out that it depends on whether the third person off at the market is still within earshot of the recitation given by the two remaining. This seems to posit a virtual community of sorts. There arguably is an echo of the human presence if the third person at the market is multi-tasking but still "present" (at least in an auditory sense) and therefore can still be considered as part of the *zimun.*

This leads me to wonder what the "echoes" of the people's face we see in our Facebook communities. Do we hear or feel enough of their presence based on past shared experiences to constitute a "friendship" whether they are friended or not? Are the people responding connected enough to warrant being considered a community? Is Facebook—full as it is of good feeling— capable of responding to the struggles and pains of those who are part of our community? (Babylonian Talmud, Tractate Berachot) (COM)

A second talmudic text: in *Pesachim* in the Jerusalem Talmud a certain Rabbi Abbahu appears somewhat mysteriously to his teacher (Rabbi Yohanan) and a group of fellow students who study under his guidance. The students notice something astounding as Abbahu moves into their visual field. His face is aglow. The Aramaic phrase used (*afu neharin*) likens the light emanating from his face to a river of light and seems to echo the experience of Moses when he received the Ten Commandments and descends from Mount Sinai emanating light (Jerusalem Talmud, Tractate *Pesachim)*.

In the text itself, the colleagues of Yohanan launch into an argument about what could cause such a glow. As scholars, they assume that it has to be somehow connected to their own learning and teaching. So they assume Abbahu must have solved some riddle of Jewish law, perhaps working his way through knotted opinions. Abbahu brings them up short however. He says he has discovered something quite small, perhaps a nuance or detail of an ancient tradition. Within this Talmudic world, every new idea has the capacity to suffuse our faces with divine light.

So I return to memories of myself teaching this very text to students in distance communities, perhaps twenty of them sharing five different quadrants of a screen. Could I possibly see their faces let alone the glow in their faces? Technology has improved and in person I now deal with smaller numbers of students. Still, is there any substitute for the human face as the full bodied appreciation of the presence of another human being?

A third Talmudic text begins with our obligation to recite the Shema, "Hear O Israel the Lord our God the Lord is One" Dt.6:5) twice daily. The question of precisely when we might say morning Shema is subject to debate. One Rabbi suggests when one hears the rooster crow. Another argues it begins when we see the first shaft of light in the morning sky. A third provides a more anthropological answer: When you can see the face of a friend.

This last answer encourages me to wonder out loud: What is the role of shadows in the appreciation of the human face? How much do we need the darker backdrop of night to fully see a face to appreciate that of a friend when it appears? That of course makes me wonder whether the bright lights and constant cascade of images on Facebook might dull our deeper appreciation for the faces of friends. Perhaps the transition from God as creator of light/God as maker of darkness reflects our need for dawn and dusk to fully humanize our appreciation of the human face. As Parker Palmer observes in *On the Brink of Everything (*Palmer,*2018, page 65)* the older we become the more our self understanding appreciates both shadow and light and the intimate relationship between the two within ourselves. Arguably, the bright lights of constantly staged photographs and selfies gets in the way of that important developmental task of growing both wiser and older.

These three texts and questions stay with me, but do not occupy me nearly as much as the fourth and fifth texts about the human face. The fourth comes from my most recent study of the French Jewish philosopher Emmanuel Levinas. The question it poses is ultimately theological and philosophical in nature.

The human face plays an essential role in Levinas's philosophy which prizes ethical obligation above logical rigor and systematic grandeur. The project of most of European philosophy over several centuries has been "essentialist," the quest for the "sameness" of our minds and souls (Kenan, 2013, introduction).

All ethical obligation comes to us from the reminders of the absolute otherness of human beings that comes only from the intrusion of the human face into our visual field. It is that face, that disruption of our predictable realities that moves us towards our deepest humanity, our most enduring ethical obligations, and our deepest relationships with God. There is no shortcut to this process. (COM)

This leads me to wonder about images and social media. Beyond the millions of unique poses, is the goal of the Facebook at its deeper levels to emphasize our sameness, our common humanity? To the extent that might be true, have we been derailed from our more enduring task in relationship to our friends, community, and ultimately to God?

Finally one notes the convergence of the theological and ethical in the opposite phenomenon, not the overly abundant presence of the "face" but its absence. Martin Buber and other Jewish philosophers have developed insights into *hastarat panim*/the disappearance of the Divine face from our lives. The absence of face, often linked to the Holocaust and other events of human suffering where one might have hoped for Divine intervention, also has hauntingly digital and ethical implications. (Buber, 2017, 100-115)

In Jewish ethical tradition we know we have shamed someone egregiously by *halvanat panim*/blanching of their face. Physiologically this whitening is the redirection of blood to some other parts of our anatomy, but rabbinic ethics attributes agency and violence to the one who causes the shaming. It is as if this draining of blood is a form of murder.

The visceral experience of seeing the impact of our hurtful words on another human being is more difficult if the person is faceless. So of course when social media platforms allow and sometimes even encourage words to be exchanged at a fast and furious rate without being able to see the "faceless" people we reference, we have entered a new world of ethical concern. Unsurprisingly, some of this new world is both anticipated in Jewish literature and documented in the world of contemporary journalism and popular psychology by Jon Ronson in *So You've Been Publicly Shamed.* (Ronson, 2015, 33-66)

## COMMENTARY

*From Rabbi Michael Cohen:* Reverend Martin Luther king, Jr. said, "All I'm saying is simply this: that all mankind is tied together; all life is interrelated, and we are all caught in an inescapable network of mutuality, tied in a single garment of destiny. Whatever affects one directly, affects all indirectly. For some strange reason I can never be what I ought to be until you are what you ought to be. And you can never be what you ought to be until I am what I ought to be - this is the interrelated structure of reality. John Donne caught it years ago and placed it in graphic terms: *No man is an Island, entire of itself; every man is a piece of the continent, a part of the main...* And then he goes on toward the end to say: *any man's death diminishes me, because I am involved in mankind; and therefore never send to know for whom the bell tolls; it tolls for thee.* And by believing this, by living out this fact, we will be able to remain awake through a great revolution."

*From Dr. Brian Amkraut:* On Rosen and "the cascading nature of Talmudic conversation": Indeed the hyperlinked world of internet information does resemble the creative web of source and commentary that characterizes talmudic study. But something critical has disappeared in the digital model, as classical talmudic study expects, perhaps even requires, that the user possess at the very least a certain level of skill and literacy with ancient, rabbinic, and medieval sources, if not a true mastery of the compendium of classical Jewish literature. Hence we surf the internet today, often with little regard for the provenance of the pages where we land and where subsequent links might take us.

*From Peter Eckstein:* In my experience as an online teacher, I have learned that if the facilitator doesn't engage the learners from afar, they will not participate. I have also found that there are learners who thrive on the facelessness of online discussion. It's as if they are freed from the chains of physicality as they participate. No one can see them. Just their words. And for many, this fosters a greater ability to articulate their thoughts and ideas.

*From Rabbi Mira Wasserman:* Hillel's response to this challenge provides insight into the larger themes of this book. For Hillel, the Torah can be summed up in a core ethical teaching: "What is hateful to you, do not do to your neighbor." But this teaching by no means exhausts Jewish learning. On the contrary, Jewish learning is infinitely expansive, and that is why the process of discovery never ends: "All the rest is commentary, go and learn!" This story tells me that while the core of Jewish teaching centers on the ethical relationship between neighbors, there are infinite ways to learn and expand on this core teaching. Technology is an important tool as we "go and learn!"

*From Amelia Gavurin:* The digital age is a gift for Jews when it comes to cultivating community. We are not all in the same village anymore and while we are blessed when we are able to be in the same physical location, the internet and all its forums and platforms allows Jews without physical community to connect, grow, and learn with other Jews.

*From Rabbi Hayim Herring:* Let's expand this question to include more space for skepticism but also hope about the shapes that community may take. Already, it's possible to purchase concert tickets to some of your favorite dead artists who perform holographically (think about the first Star Wars movie, where Princess Leia appears as a 3-D holograph, sending a message for help). Is that "creepy" or a way to enjoy an experience with a community of fans who appreciate a certain artist? When we reach the technological tipping point where immersive experiences are so real that we can make eye contact, shake hands, and smell freshly ground coffee in a digital meeting space, will that heighten, diminish, or transform our "mistrust" of community? And, what about connecting with community vertically, meaning that those who come after us won't be limited to looking at our two-dimensional pictures or videos, but can hear us, see us, and be present with us at family celebrations or holidays? Does that add or detract to creating a kehillah kedoshah/community of holiness?

And now we find ourselves caught with a paradox of having more apps to communicate but fewer skills to do so—what I have named "social in-app-titude." In part, it's because our visual field is limited to a handheld or wearable device. Looking at the "face" of a smartwatch, or being seduced by apps like "FaceTime," don't replace the experience of having a face-to-face conversation that requires eye contact with "the other." Younger people can search for information at blinding speed, but they won't understand attributes like resilience, courage, and compassion from a Google search. At the same time, those of us who are slower with our thumbs can be more open to learning from younger generations who lack experience, but who have fascinating perspectives. We have solutions to models of mutual mentoring in the Bible. The Levites had a mandatory retirement age of 50, but there is a debate about when their service began: at age 25 or 30 (compare Numbers 4:3 and Numbers 8:24–26 in which different ages for starting Levitical service are given). One resolution to this question is that they had a five-year period of mentorship before they entered service and once the mandatory retirement age was reached, the older Levites still got to eat with the younger ones. Did the younger Levites discuss new ways or technologies of offering the sacrifices while still within the bounds of tradition, and did retired Levites share their initial experiences of service with those who were just beginning? On a different note, why were members of every generation invited to participate at the gathering at which the entire Torah was read every seven years

(Deut. 31:10-13)? What does that teach us about the value of each generation having its own unique contributions to make to the other during that shared experience?

*From Rabbi Steven Sager:* Social media can dilute the nature of friendship. The abundance of shared information, including photos and videos, does not breach the gap of experience. The Hebrew poet, Zelda, recognizes that even immediate friendship has its distances:

*Standing near the gate is as much*
*as the comforters can bear. Even my soul is miles away*
*from the crying 'I.'* (Zelda, "Don't Be Far")

*From Peter Eckstein:* I think the what, how and with whom we communicate in today's virtual world reflects the idea of identity plasticity mentioned earlier. The way we communicate with one another IRL is very different then via 120 character tweets or FaceBook posts, or SMS messages. Each of these technologies forces us to change who we are. Think about twitter handles or Facebook profiles or LinkedIn bios. What are we marketing? To whom? Why?

*From Rabbi Nathan Kamesar:* I struggle with this, too, but I've ultimately come down on the side of allowing the market to determine which forms of media are in demand. While I sometimes lament the notion that "no one reads books anymore" I'm not sure this is really true. Book sales are up over the last several years, and I've noticed an increase in demand for longform journalism. There has also been a proliferation of audiobooks and podcasts for those who are more auditorily driven. I think that while surely some of us get sucked into the brevity and the addictive nature of media like Twitter, it has its own time and place (for me, while watching live events like sports or debates), and books and other long reads also hold a necessary place in my life. I trust people to feel the pull of deeper learning alongside their more immediate, short-term yearning for content.

*From Dr. Mary Hess:* We are living in an age of "networked individualism." That framework (from Rainey and Wellman) has been drawn on by Campbell, to list characteristics of religion in this kind of space. She lists six: Networked Community (loosely-bounded social networks), Storied Identity (fluid & dynamic identity construction), Shifting Authority (Simultaneous empowerment & challenge of authority), Convergent Practice (personalized blending of information & rituals), and Multi-site Reality (embedded online-offline connections). (Campbell, Journal of the American Academy of Religion, pp. 1–30doi:10.1093/jaarel/lfr074)

My entire academic career has been spent arguing that theological education is both deeply embodied AND possible to pursue in digital media. The usual argument is that theological education is a thoroughly embodied exercise and digital media are a disembodying practice. To which my usual response is: I, as a woman in theological education, have often been in theological classrooms where my embodied presence has been deliberately ignored, I have been "disembodied," if you will. While in many digital spaces I am empowered to be much more fully present in all of my embodied selfhood.

Parker Palmer observed: "of course, the spiritual concept of grace goes beyond 'information' and 'events' into a realm of relational mystery that is at the heart of the way of knowing and teaching described in this book. In receiving spiritual grace we understand that we not only seek but are sought, that we not only known but are known, that we not only love but are loved.... it is a gift we cannot manipulate and command but for which we can only pray." (p. 113, To Know As We Are Known)

The human face—which our brain grants so much importance to that we have a separate part of our brain devoted to its visual recognition—is still not seen by some people. My own son lives with the challenge of prosopagnosia (face blindness), and it has been digital tech which has supported him into real relationships he otherwise might not have. So digital tech is—as you have pointed out—simultaneously—many things. (MH)

The paradox that we are both free to experience the love and grace of our humanity in ways never before possible AND that the public performance of hatred has been deeply enhanced is an insight first shared by Michael Wesch, an anthropologist of the net (https://youtu.be/TPAO-lZ4_hU). Christianity—like many religious traditions—lives deeply into paradox. It is at the heart of our convictions about God being both divine and human, of God being Three and One, of human beings being both "saint" and "sinner" Indeed, I think it likely that it is our religious traditions that have the most to offer us by way of contemplative and unitive (but not uniform) ways to engage the deep mysteries of our existence which are newly visible because of digital tech.

I am so conscious of this in my own work! We know that digital media reshape how we understand authority, what we mean by authenticity, how we experience agency. Digital media highlight personal, individual agency—often in very creative ways. But lost in all of the human invention is awareness of, gratitude for, respect for God's agency in the midst of Creation. It's crucial to invite persons back into that deep relationship with transcendence.

Dear Evolving Self (Dear Jeffrey, Dear Commentator),

*Chapter Thirteen*

# Congregations in the Digital Age: Four Frames and a Half Dozen Creative Congregational Initiatives

**SELF-AWARENESS**, balance, and perspective

Synagogues and all faith communities need to move with kavana, great intentionality, into the mainstream of the digital age. Such movement requires a sharp sense of what it means for organizations to evolve and change planfully. There is no shortage of volumes by scholars like Isa Aron and Ron Wolfson documenting what it means for a synagogue to embrace change in a deep way. It is less common for this analysis to deal specifically with technology though one finds a notable exception in the work of Terri Elton and Hayim Herring on social media in congregational life (Elton and Herring, 2016, 173–186). It is entirely common that technology, or more particularly, the lack of good technology is the focus of a lament from those who plan the Jewish future—why don't we do more of it and do it better! To my mind this lament is one-sided.

Before we explore what a fully and thoughtfully engaged digital synagogue might look like, we might recognize the complexity of the synagogue as an organization. Bolman and Deal are among those who help us plan from a matrix of complexity in their model of organizations operating in four distinct, yet overlapping realms: the structural, the symbolic, the political, and the human resource (https://bigthink.com/bolman-deal-frameworks) The lead concerns in each of these realms is listed below:

Structural: This Frame focuses on the obvious 'how' of change. It's mainly a task-orientated Frame. It concentrates on strategy; setting measurable goals, clarifying task, responsibilities and reporting lines; agreeing metrics and deadlines; and creating systems and procedures.

Human Resources: The Human Resource (HR) Frame places more emphasis on people's needs. It primarily focuses on giving employees the power and opportunity to perform their jobs well, while at the same time, addressing their needs for human contact, personal growth, and job satisfaction.

Political: The Political Frame addresses the problem of individuals and interest groups having sometimes conflicting (often hidden) agendas, especially at times when budgets are limited and the organisation have to make difficult choices. In this Frame you will see coalition-building, conflict resolution work, and power-base building to support the leader's initiatives. (COM)

Symbolic: The Symbolic Frame addresses people's needs for a sense of purpose and meaning in their work. It focuses on inspiring people by making the organisation's direction feel significant and distinctive. It includes creating a motivating vision, and recognising superb performance through company celebrations.

## STRUCTURAL

The structural frame will demand of a synagogue clarity about the values it most cherishes. Strategies will also need to be in place for guiding the values from ideas into practice. A good starting place comes from the "evolve" series of Reconstructing Judaism in an article on harnessing technology by Rabbis Nathan Kamesar and Deborah Waxman where they suggest the following list of relevant Jewish values (http://evolve.reconstructingjudaism .org/harnessingtechnology)

*Ki gerim hayitem/remember that you were strangers (and how this teaches us the importance of empathy)*
*Tochekhah/sacred rebuke*
*Kedushah/holiness*
*Tzelem Elohim/we are each created in the divine image*
*Kol yisrael arevim zeh bazeh/our deep interconnectedness*
*Ahavah rabah/there exists an expansive universal love we can draw upon*
*Shabbat; shvitah/rest*
*Panim el panim/Buber's principles of genuine dialogue*
*Leshem shamayim/importance that arguments must be for the sake of Heaven*
*Kavod/ethical privacy practices*
*Tzedek tzedek tirdof; tikun olam/pursuit of justice*
*Im shamoa tishma/sacred listening*
*Sichat brit/covenantal conversation*

Let's imagine that there is a working task force on technology for our synagogue. Technical and ethical expertise, Jewish knowledge and technological savvy are all well represented within the group. There is no shortage of techniques available from the worlds of planning and organizational management to suggest how this group might proceed. Beyond these specific techniques an awareness of values based decision making guides the Jewish work of the committee.

As just one example, the group might utilize some combination of appreciative inquiry and a force field analysis to explore their values. The first step would be to focus on several of the most critical values related to the current life of the congregation. Then, appreciative inquiry approach would point us toward new resources and possibilities while celebrating what is already digitally a force for good within the congregation. The force field analysis would have the group look more critically at the ways in which the intersection of synagogue life and the digital world both actualize and impede these values.

I can imagine the group choosing one value each year as a focus of deep study and assessment of its contemporary status in our digital lives. Such action research should also lead to a set of suggested future initiatives the congregation might take to more fully integrate the positive sides of technology as they relate to the identified value.


## SYMBOLIC

Our relationship to digital life is embedded in a lattice of larger assumptions about human beings and their relationship to tools and technology. As Thomas Friedman notes, even as we place the world in our hands with our smartphones, there is a world within us that interprets what such a powerful tool means to us. We need to play what Stephen Brookfield calls "the assumption hunting game" to flesh out these implicit epistemological and valuational commitments (Brookfield, 2012, chapter five.)

Shabbat is one such arena that is symbolically charged. In chapter four we explored how different philosophical and Jewish worldviews might affect the way we limit or allow for the use of technology on the Jewish Sabbath. In chapter nine we explored the way in which one of our primary civilizations might lead to an affirmative use of technology on Shabbat and the other, our Jewish tradition, might argue in a different direction. How we maintain and balance the tensions between our most deeply held values is also part of the story.

If the Sabbath provides a model of the symbolic world in time, the architecture of the synagogue provides an arena for exploring how these symbols are embodied in space. In chapter three of this volume we explored the Chasidic text about the importance of paradox and its implications for our relationship to technology. This should be reflected in the synagogue building itself. These days one finds a few computers in our synagogues' education wing, symbolically indicating that a child's Jewish education should be connected to our digital world. These resources are seriously underutilized, but the larger issue is that adults are equally part of the digital world. My ideal synagogue technology lab would be full of wonderful digital resources and devices for adults to playfully learn as well.

The other side of the paradox, however, is also reflected in our buildings. There are several rooms for meditation and small group dialogue that are by design without computer connections. A refined artistic aesthetic in the sculpting of physical space makes these rooms places to unplug, read a wonderful book, and meditate.

## POLITICAL

Political stakeholders need to respect each others' ideas and values. In the digital landscape there are many competing stakeholders and winners and losers, including who has access to new digital tools and who does not. From the standpoint of *ledor vador* and Jewish continuity no tensions are more worthy of creative resolution than those pertaining to digital natives and digital immigrants discussed in chapter seven. While humor courses through Prensky's presentation of the distinction in chapter seven. I have often seen digital immigrants near tears when they have a chance to express their feelings about being left in the technological backwash. Serious generational tensions exist across the divide. (COM)

I am not aware of any precise metrics for measuring whether the tension between digital natives and immigrants is more than sometimes funny and sometimes seriously annoying. From a Jewish/religious perspective I am convinced that in an era that hungers for stronger connection between the generations, creatively addressing this issue can lead to creative and impactful strategies. I am presently working with several synagogues on a program I call the "wisdom/skills" exchange as a way of fostering deeper connection between generations. In this program "immigrants"(sometimes, but not always parents) are invited to meet with "natives" (teens) and engage in a significant cultural exchange. The natives come to the meeting with a full supply of apps and technology tips that will help their senior immigrants creatively enhance their ability to utilize technology. In exchange, the natives are presented with stories from the immigrants about ethical and cultural challenges they have faced over the course of a lifetime and the wisdom they have developed.

## HUMAN RESOURCES FRAME

I have just returned from a meeting of Twin Cities Jew Folk, a dynamic and growing Minneapolis-St. Paul group of communities designed to reach millennial and gen z populations ( https://tcjewfolk.com/) Quite sensibly they have tried to position themselves within the digital generation gap, utilizing a grant to offer congregation free advice about properly implementing social media platforms. This consultation to the largely "immigrant" leadership population of synagogues might otherwise amount to astronomical fees paid to an outside consulting firm. Such external outsourcing also runs the risk of relying on media experts who do not know the Jewish world they are serving. Now in addition to a more conventional IT person synagogues have access to a social media consultant. What is missing from the bank of human/professional resources? I imagine the development of a "HIT", a *chokhmah/wisdom* internet technology person. In my vision this person is a highly trained, paid member of the professional staff. Her work is triggered in part by following up on a new synagogue tradition. Each year around the fall holidays every synagogue member receives a set of the newest digital resources for Jewish learning and living. Not all, but many, congregants are eager to meet with the HIT person to follow up the gift and customize these resources.

The role of this HIT person would be multi-faceted. She also would partner with a congregational psychologist to facilitate a reading/support group that discusses Adam Alter's *Irresistible*, a volume focusing on the epidemic of smartphone and other digital addictions. Finally, this human resource gem, would also partner with the synagogues building committee to make sure that the plans for a new synagogue spaces include both digital wonderlands for fully engaging technology, and peaceful oases that are totally unplugged, by community design and sanction.

## COMMENTARY

*From Reverend Teri Elton:* The symbolic frame centers on making meaning, especially in the midst of complexities. Stories, rituals, and art are some ways the symbolic frame is lived out. Given this reality, what does it mean for us that digital tools tell stories, are connected with rituals, and use/create art? As we live in complex times, this frame has an increased importance. Therefore it seems right to discover ways to bring technology into this process. If we do not, people will be left to make meaning of related to technology in a vacuum without a community.

The same can be said of other divides. Digital tools are fueled by power that multiplies as it is shared. As we live in an increasingly diverse world, where old structures have become obstacles for new voices and/or marginalized persons, social platforms and digital technology has opened up new avenues for new conversations, relationships, and learning that is diverse and more egalitarian. This is something communities of faith can capitalize on and engage.

Dear Evolving Self (Dear Jeffrey, Dear Commentator),

*Part IV*

# COMING FULL CIRCLE

# A Personal Perspective on Rabbi Joseph Soloveitchik's Adam I and Adam II in the Digital Age

**SELF-AWARENESS,** balance, perspective

I'd like to return to elements of my own story as a learning Jewish human being as I move towards a more personal stance in my relationship to technology. Here I will be extending and expanding some comments from Chapter Five about Rabbi Soloveitchik's *Lonely Man of Faith*. Some of my own "greening" and growing environmentalism over time will also be apparent.

In 1969, as I was finishing a year studying in Israel, I received some bad news. There had been a huge oil spill off the Santa Barbara coast. The scenes of oil soaked birds mixed in my mind with sweeter pictures of the Santa Barbara beaches that had been the playground for my meeting and falling in love with my wife Deborah when we were both undergraduate students at the University of California at Santa Barbara.

Later, I would come to appreciate some significant good that came out of this environmental disaster. After focusing on the external idiosyncrasies of the event (who "plans" an oil spill?) deeper and more structural issues were addressed. The EPA was formed in response to disasters like this and the burning of the Cuyahoga River in Cleveland. Profundity added to the philosophy of environmentalism by the powerful concept of "the tragedy of the commons" as developed by Garrett Hardin, then a professor at University of California at Santa Barbara.

My first response, however, was all pain and emotion. *My* beach had been spoiled. To the extent that I could place any cognitive frame around it at all, I remembered a meeting of religious theologians at Claremont College in 1967. The group proclaimed baldly that the "Judaeo-Christian" tradition of elevating humans above the rest of creation (as "commanded" in Genesis 1:28), was at the heart of the impending crisis in our relationship to the natural world.

The triumph of Soloveitchik's Adam I—the majestic Adam who ruled the rest of creation—had created quite a mess for us all.

In my rabbinic and religious studies I came to learn of Christian traditions of stewardship and Jewish concepts of being God's partners in maintaining the world of nature that softened this judgment. Yet, I still feel some version of that revulsion to this very day. Last year I heard an echo of the potential impact of such crass materialism in David Brooks' book *The Road to Character*. Brooks argued in this volume that we need to move away from (or at least better balance) the "resume virtues" so naturally aligned with Adam I to the "eulogy virtues" in our character that only the Adam II can understand and cultivate. Deep caring for the environment is certainly one of those eulogy virtues.

I have also developed a deeper appreciation of what I believe was Soloveitchik's intent in developing the portraits of Adam I and Adam II. To repeat what was underscored in Chapter Five, the two Adams are not two different human beings or mere archetypes but real forces that live with creative tension inside each of us. I offer below an example drawn from my everyday routine.

I engage aspects of both Adam I and Adam II several times a week at my fitness center. They both have a place in my fifty minutes on the bicycle. Adam I is there for the first thirty minutes when I set very clear goals to achieve, benchmarks to eclipse and conquer. I want to keep going at 90 rpm through all but the most severe of the rolling hills. It feels good to achieve that goal and master the routine.

Then it is time to shift gears both physically and metaphorically. The particular bike I use has a scenic function. I take several deep breaths and create a thought bubble. I sweep into it all the random, distracting thinking of the day. I pop the bubble and take seven deep breaths following the rhythm of reciting *yud-hey-vav hey* (the four syllables of one of God's Hebrew names). Then, while maintaining a reasonable speed, I allow myself to move inside the pictures on the screen. I am then walking across a mountain stream, hiking around the Minneapolis lakes, circling Stonehenge. I am not changing or conquering the scenery. My ecological intelligence that apprehends the universe with wonder does this fairly effortlessly. I am deploying the gifts of the Adam II in my nature. (COM)

In an important way, Adam II specializes in the gift of connectedness. "Connectedness," however, is a mansion of many different rooms. This becomes obvious in a series of sentences created by my eighth graders at Heilicher Minneapolis Jewish Days as they began to explore the way digital life expands our connections. Their prompt was to share two sentences in which the word "connected" appeared. Their uncurated set of sentences include:

Why do you feel such a connection with me.

The pair of conjoined twins was connected at the waist.

Sometimes my wifi is not connected.

My keyboard is connected to my wifi.

Magnets connect to other magnets.

I love to connect with my friends outside school.

I'm very connected to sports.

I love this book so much because I feel connected to the characters.

I connected with my family on a trip to national parks.

There is a connection between Minnesota and Canada is that they both love hockey.

I am connected to the polleverywhere account.

I feel connected to the Heilicher community.

The class analyzed their sentences for content and structure. They were given flashcards for *peshat*/concrete meaning and *derash*/metaphoric meaning. They held up the appropriate card as each sentence was read indicating whether "connected" was, in their judgment, functioning concretely or metaphorically. A deeper discussion began about which forms of connection are more trivial and which more meaningful.

As this conversation unfolded I thought very much about Sherry Turkle's insights that digital life puts connection on steroids. We are terrified of not connecting, of not being "friended" on Facebook or followed on Twitter. I am also reminded of the work of the psychoanalyst Andras Angyal (Angyal, 1973, Introduction) who found it important to detail the twin, equally intense human urges for autonomy and differentiation on the one hand and for homonymy and joining together on the other. The prevailing cultural wisdom of the 1950's and 60's privileged autonomy, hence the oddness of the very term "homonomy" Angyal sought to introduce. Yet, now the weight has possibly swung back in the other directions, largely because of all the connections offered by our online culture.

Turkle illuminates this phenomenon in a penetrating way. Our desire for connection is deep and enduring. In the endless world of possibilities of Facebook friends, twitter followers, and instagram viewers this phenomenon of connection is clearly intensified. In fact, it touches the very core of our being. We begin to measure ourselves by the number of connections we have made or the number of people who have liked us or friended us. We run the danger of a barely conscious quantitative metric overcoming quality conversations and connections in our own sense of self-worth and dignity.

This phenomenon is particularly challenging for teenagers but is present for all of us. It leads to what she characterizes in *Alone Together* as the

Goldilocks effect, a desire to be connected but in a very controlled, mediated, "just right" way. We never want to lose touch, we fear our "aloneness" but we paradoxically fear drawing too close as well (among other things who could manage so many in depth connections). We create a new categorical imperative for shaping who we are. No longer are we Descartes', "I think therefore I am" or the Dutch theologian Jans Huizinga's "I play therefore I am". Our new category is, "I share therefore I am".

To share well and to merge ourselves with multiple communities is an art and in the digital age a special challenge as well. I think Adam I has some gifts to offer in this dizzying, new world of endless possibile connections. As a necessary concomitant of Adam I's gaining mastery in the world, he has developed a storehouse of analytic thinking powers. That is how Adam I becomes a paragon of science, engineering, and rational thinking.

Our challenge today is to "ethicize" those analytic powers of Adam I and use them not as means of conquest, but as tools of self-awareness. We need Adam I to rise in service of forming ethical judgments about all the new forms of connectedness so naively embraced by the Adam II of our nature.

This very act of keeping our collective Adam I focused on the ethical side of his gifts performs one other critical function. Adam I possesses great gifts of focus and single-mindedness. She does not, however, multitask very well. More attention to the ethical analysis of connection means less time for Adam I to express her love of achievement and conquest over the natural world.

Cleary, the needs of our time require Adam I to engage in such a self-transformation. We are near the tipping point where we must turn a classical midrash on its head. In *Bereshit Rabbah*, the rabbinic commentary on the book of Genesis, the Rabbis have God share with us the good news: We have been given a beautiful world to enjoy and guard. With the good news comes the bad news: We will be gifted only one such world.

We have endangered this precious world and have a shorter and shorter timetable for saving it. My colleague and teacher Rabbi Arthur Waskow once observed that the term global warming is misleading. In our minds, "warm" things evoke images of warm and cuddly. What we really have is "global scorching". Cooling off this trend in the deepest psychological and spiritual ways can only occur if the dialectical tensions between Adam I and Adam II our recalibrated with a clear intent on addressing this deepening environmental crisis.

As I complete this chapter I have also just finished the "Israel Ride." The Israel Ride is a 200 mile, five day ride from Jerusalem to Eilat in support of Hazon, the Jewish sustainability lab and the Arava Institute, a group that under the banner of "nature knows no borders" brings together Israeli Jews, Israeli Arabs, Palestinians, Jordanians, and diaspora Jews to study common environmental problems. In doing some teaching with the beautiful landscape of the *aravah*/Israeli wilderness as backdrop I realized that there is a simpler way to put all this. The biblical description of Yom Kippur has us sending off our sins via a goat to the wilderness. We need to say the same to the excessive sides of Adam I *lech l'azazel* (leave us; off to the wilderness with you) in order to grant ourselves the moratorium, the gift of time, to truly address environmental issues in a most serious way.

## COMMENTARY

*From Rabbi Michael Cohen:* Adam I asks, How? Adam II asks, Why? We need to ask both questions.

Dear Evolving Self (Dear Jeffrey, Dear Commentator),

# Waiting for Elijah: *Machlakot/* Enduring Controversies that Matter, What We Yet Need to Know about Our Relationships to Technology

**PERSPECTIVE,** self-awareness, balance

Elijah the prophet uses the most advanced technology of his time, a flaming chariot, to exit this world (Kings II, chapter 1) and move on to _____? Well, we are never told where he went. This is precisely why Elijah is such an enigmatic figure. The mystery of his life's ending has inspired many generations of Jewish storytellers to speculate about how and when he will return. In fact, storytellers of all faiths are intrigued by this figure. One Shabbat evening we had our son's boss and his wife as guests in our Minneapolis home. Daren and his wife Sharisa are devout Mormons who live in Salt Lake City. Being good hosts we introduced them to everyone in our family.... two kids, three grandkids, in-laws... and last but not least to our turtle Elijah.

We call him Elijah because he came into our lives unexpectedly, literally dropped on our doorstep by someone who saw a note about our having lost a different turtle (Turtle-Turtle by name) in Shaker Heights, Ohio. Elijah was not that Turtle but he has been with us for seven years now. His aquarium sits right by our dinner table. He is an unusually gregarious turtle—and while that might be human projection—it is empirical fact that we can see him from the dinner table.

Having introduced our guests to Elijah we were quite ready to move on to other topics. Yet our guests wanted to keep on talking about Elijah. Were we aware they asked, somewhat rhetorically, that in Mormon thought Elijah (the prophet not the turtle) plays a very critical role? It is Elijah who is said to have entrusted Joseph Smith, founding prophet of the Latter Day Saints, with the keys to the new sanctuary which would become the spiritual center for their new Zion.

We in fact did not know that, but were not totally surprised because the character of Elijah is full of surprises. In fact he is a wonderful figure to consider in our digital twenty-first century. According to Rabbinic lore, Elijah travels with lightning-like speed and can seemingly appear out of nowhere to perform a new mitzvah/good deed for someone in need. He thus is well suited to keep pace with the fast paced changes of the digital age! (Shramm, 1997, 1–7)

Elijah does not flinch at delivering a stern prophetic message, yet tenderly welcomes newborn Jewish babies into the covenant of the people Israel. He is multi-faced in the disguises he wears while doing this work. He puts the avatars of Second Life to shame in terms of his ability to reinvent himself. Elijah is also the healer of lost connections between the generations, the one who according to the prophet Malachi "turns the hearts of the children to their parents, and the parents to their children", offering hope for bridging any digital divide between immigrants and natives.

For the purposes of this volume, the two most relevant features of Elijah lie elsewhere, however. According to Hasidic lore, Elijah is not just an external figure. Each of us has within us *koach eliyahu*/Elijah power (Wiener, 1978, introduction). This power helps us to do good deeds but also to think deeply and creatively about our place in the world. My humble hope is that this volume has helped the reader make some sense of the extraordinary digital world that envelops us. If so, I give all credit to the reader's Elijah power. My role was only to frame the questions.

Elijah is also the prophet who has the responsibility of figuring out answers to questions that have proven too difficult for even the most inventive human minds. Periodically, in the Talmud one will see the acronym TEIKU which stands for the Hebrew phrase Elijah will settle all problems that have proven irresolvable through rabbinic debate. The same phrase is used today in contemporary Hebrew to indicate a tie in a soccer game. Undoubtedly most Israeli soccer fans have no consciousness of this particular double entendre of the Hebrew language with its religious and theological rumblings beneath the surface.

So it is entirely appropriate that as this volume moves towards its end it does so on a characteristically Jewish note, mixing *hutzpah* and humility. Below I have the temerity to make a few suggestions to my Elijah avatar:

Can we reshape the way technology shapes us?

What does Judaism contribute to our Digital Lives?

What kinds of sacred technologies of growth can help us best manage the paradox of both over and underutilizing technology?

Is there a *dayenu*/it is enough song to be sung to our technological selves?

Elijah has many helpers in this world and I hope Elijah would approve of my ending by calling on three individuals whom I believe are full of *koach eliyahu*/Elijah power in order to ask important questions in the future (knowing that the ultimate answers are Elijah's alone to provide): Marshall Mcluhan, Tom Friedman, and Martin Buber.

Question # 1 Can We Reshape the Tools that Have Shaped Us?

Marshall McLuhan suggests that the very notion of agency is shaped by our technology. The title of his most seminal volume is <u>not</u> the *Medium is the* **Message** but the *Medium is the* **Massage**. The technologically driven emerging global village is linked to the way different media shape our bodies and senses. Radio privileges the ear and the auditory system; television the totality of our senses. For the Renaissance person the eye leads to the amusing illustration in the book of perfect symmetry and balance and McLuhan's quip that the motto of the Renaissance was "every man in his Piazza, and a Piazza for every man".

McLuhan's insights suggest a soft form of technological determinism easily linked to the explosion of research in neuroscience and the notion of neuroplasticity. The human brain can be shaped in innumerable directions because of its very plasticity. I want to keep an open mind in understanding technology not as message and technique but as a total sensory massage of who we are. This means that though we answer positively the question of whether we can reshape the tools that shape us we also retain a heightened meta-awareness of how this process unfolds.

In the recently released animated children's film "Ralph Who Wrecked the Internet," we see an interesting portrayal of the relationship between ourselves and our technology. Our technologies and our deepest selves are in constant interplay with one another. They constitute a double feedback loop. The virus that ultimately infects computers worldwide is Ralph's own self-doubts and need to prop himself up by controlling his deepest relationships.

We cannot simply step outside of our surrounding influences to some transcending platform of rational decision-making to examine our digital lives. We need—as I have argued throughout the volume—sophisticated tools of self-awareness, perspective, and balance in order to find and anchor ourselves while we simultaneously move within the digital universe. I have tried to provide at least a few of these tools. (COM)

Question #2: What does Judaism contribute to our Digital Life?

Tom Friedman's volume *Thank You for Being Late: An Optimist's Guide to Thriving in the Age of Accelerations* surveys the three revolutions that characterize twenty-first century life: bubbling, seemingly inexhaustible opportunities for entrepreneurship; the technological revolution occasioned by the smart phone where the world is in our hand; and the green revolution of environmental concern and activism. Near the end of the volume he asks what it takes to fully embrace the winged adventures of each of these revolutions? He provides his own answer in terms of the roots in community that are needed to anchor these accelerations. As John Mickelthwait writes in his 2016 New York Times review:

> Once there, he tries to see the community for what it was and is, all the while looking for the source of its still-evident civic spirit—and for lessons that can be replicated in communities across the country. The story of St. Louis Park, he writes, "is the story of how an ethic of pluralism and a healthy community got built one relationship, one breakup, one makeup, one insult, one welcoming neighbor, one classroom at a time." While nostalgia is certainly a factor in this rosy assessment, there's more to his trip down memory lane and explorations of what happens in a community where people take the time to get to know each other and build bonds across their differences—or, as he puts it, who are willing "to belong to a network of intertwined 'little platoons', communities of trust, which [form] the foundation for belonging, for civic idealism, for believing others who [are different] [can] and should belong, too." Yes, in an age of accelerating global interdependence and contact between strangers, "the bridges of understanding that we have to build are longer, the chasms they have to span much deeper." But that is the challenge.

In my own simpler words, we human beings are indeed always striving for both roots and wings. One can hardly provide a better challenge for Jewish tradition. The balance between roots and wings is arguably the Jewish story writ large.

Question #3: How do we manage the paradox of both under and over utilizing technology?

Here I would direct the reader to the website of *Text Me: Ancient Jewish Wisdom Meets Contemporary Technology* (textmejudaism.com.) *This* goal cannot be reduced to words and formulas but requires ongoing searching and exploration. The website is designed to provide a platform for this exploration.

Question #4: Is there a *dayenu*/enough song to be sung to our technological selves?

Martin Buber's poem *Love and Power* provides us with a worthy last word about our ability to live noble spiritual and ethical lives in the digital age

The poem reads:

*Every morning*
*I shall concern myself anew about the boundary*
*Between the love-deed-Yes and the power-deed-No*
*And pressing forward honor reality.*
*We cannot avoid*
*Using power,*
*Cannot escape the compulsion*
*To afflict the world,*
*So let us, cautious in diction*
*And mighty in contradiction,*
*Love powerfully.*
*Martin Buber, in "Power and Love",* (Friedman, 1969, 73)

How can we love powerfully, spiritually, and ethically are amazing digital lives?

Dear Evolving Self (Dear Jeffrey, Dear Commentator),

*Chapter Sixteen, Reprise III*

# Making T.S. Eliot Happy... Coming Back to Where We Began our Journey and Seeing It for the First Time

**SELF-AWARENESS,** balance, perspective

It is time now to offer readers the opportunity to reflect on what new insights might have come their way in the course of reading this volume. In the introduction, I made a commitment to utilize my own insights and understandings to offer the reader the gifts of **self-awareness, perspective and balance.** Now we must see if the reader and writer have together realized the potential of this promise. We return to these three gifts and the questions that might allow for one final exploration of our relationships to technology.

## GIFT ONE: SELF-AWARENESS

1. What new insights have I gained about my own relationship to technology?
2. When is technology a pure gift for me? When is it a conditional gift? When is it a problematic gift?
3. What new potential for Jewish learning does digital life provide for me and my family? How might I now act on the potential?
4. When 98% of this volume has either evaporated or gone into deep storage, what 2% do I want to keep alive?

## GIFT TWO: THE GIFT OF PERSPECTIVE, *SIYAG*/FENCE

1. What do I now see differently about the digital seas that surround me?
2. Can I trace the footprints of various new technologies on my everyday habits as they have evolved over time?

3. Where does my relationship to technology differ from generations older and younger than me?
4. If I think of myself as always striving to become a GJGDC (Good Jewish Global Digital Citizen) where would I give myself the highest and lowest grades in regard to each of the letters?
5. As a teacher/educator or a parent/educator how do I help my children/ grandchildren become good Jewish global digital citizens?
6. As a spiritual leader (rabbi, priest, minister, or imam) how do I raise these kinds of questions with my congregation?
7. What rhythm have I created for myself in balancing healthy engagement and healthy disengagement from my devices?

### GIFT THREE: THE GIFT OF BALANCE: THE FOUR CHASIDIC NOTES IN MY POCKET (ELEVATED HUMAN DIGNITY, HUMILITY, EXPANSIVE NEW USES OF TECHNOLOGY, LIMITING TECHNOLOGY IN MY LIFE)

1. Do I find comfortable and meaningful the way in which technology expands my sense of self?
2. Do I feel comfortable and meaningful the way in which technology "humbles" me?
3. In what ways have I utilized technology to promote my own Jewish learning journey?
4. In what ways can technology still move me forward in that journey?
5. What might I say to my own children and grandchildren as part of an ethical will bequeathing my life experience and wisdom about technology to the next generation?
6. What resolutions about technology in my life would I like to make as part of a more comprehensive *cheshbon hanefesh/soul inventory* next Rosh Hashanah and Yom Kippur?
7. What kind of deeper, more continuous connection with family and friends can be enhanced through technology? (TMW)

Returning to the first chapter the reader might also revisit the five stances towards technology (adaptive navigator, early adopter, heroic resistor educated consumer, and moderator). Has the reader shifted at all in terms of which stands embody his own values? What position would be most enriching and meaningful to adapt looking forward to the next five years of her life? (TMW)

Finally, one might step back and follow the lead of a famous Jewish liturgical poem about the Sabbath, *Lecha Dodi*. The poem begins *shamor vezachor bedibur echad,* remember and act as if they were a single word: What echoes of dissonances and synergies does the reader now hear in the imperative "Text Me!" if it were indeed a single exhortation?

Through the miracle of communication technology the author (Rabbi Jeffrey Schein) invites readers to share with him the unasked questions that might yet be part of a revised edition of this volume a few years down the road. Be in touch with him at utschein@gmail.com and share your own questions, ideas, and challenges. With your permission, some of these will be posted on the Text Me: Ancient Jewish Wisdom Meets Contemporary Technology website to stimulate, challenge, and comfort others. Your last word in response to the volume might be one of the first words for our website and the ongoing dialogue about these critical issues.

Dear Evolving Self (Dear Jeffrey, Dear Commentator),

## Chapter Seventeen

# *Lehayim:* Pittsburgh and New Zealand Postscript

(Author's Note: I was born and raised in the Squirrel Hill section of Pittsburgh. My first synagogue was the Tree of Life synagogue and over the years I have consulted with the Dor Hadash Reconstructionist congregation which sustained the loss of one member and serious injury to a second person as a result of the October 27th shooting)

Imagine three initially parallel arcs bending towards one another in unpredictable ways along the space-time continuum. One arc is the history of technology, a complex set of events beginning with the discovery of gunpowder by Chinese scientist-healers around 850 C.E. and culminating (for now) with the advent of the AR-15 automatic machine gun.

Along a second arc, find the history of *homo sapiens* attempting to humanize their own technological ingenuity, developing regulations regarding the allowed, permitted, encouraged, and outlawed uses of technology. A third arc representing the incredible recent history of digital technologies, particularly those of social media as a form of connection and communication is also at play.

Whether or not these three arcs may separate and reconnect in the future, they certainly came together in a powerful way on Saturday October 27th in the Squirrel Hill section of Pittsburgh, Pennsylvania. A gunman brimming over with hatred for Jews attacked *Tree of Life* synagogue and killed 11 Jews that morning with an AR-15 weapon. Beyond any reasonable doubt, a good deal of that hatred was fueled by the killer's participation in various social media platforms.

Meanwhile, thousands of people in Pittsburgh and hundreds of thousands around the world used social media to cope with the immediate and long range effects of the attack. People confirmed the death or safety of loved ones, friends, and acquaintances. Long dormant friendships and family relationships were reignited by concerns for the safety of people estranged by time and distance. People received solace and comfort from one another. Digital cemeteries and houses of shiva (grieving forums) emerged. Within a matter of days, systematic digital grids of *hesed*/caring allowed people to assure that families affected by the tragedy would have meals provided for months.

This tale of tragedy and humane response also illustrates the larger story of this volume. Digital technology places us simultaneously in an age of heightened danger and enhanced humanity. How might we bend the vectors of the three intersecting arcs so as to minimize the danger and maximize the human good?

With an even greater poignancy given the events that transpired in Christchurch, New Zealand this past week that mirror this same analysis, I end this book with a seemingly trite but nonetheless important selection from Deuteronomy, the fifth book of the Jewish Torah. We learn in Deuteronomy that God has placed the power of life and death in our hands. Our holy task is in all instances to "choose life "(*uvacharta chayim*)!

Dear Evolving Self (Dear Jeffrey, Dear Commentator),

# Appendix A: Guide for Different Readers

As indicated in the introduction this book is designed to leave open spaces for individual reader's questions and reflections at their own pace. However, it is also likely that various affinity groups will want to devote a period of time to the volume in a more structured way. Below are some suggestions of how to tailor the reading and dialogue to their particular roles and interests.

## ADULT BOOK CLUBS AND READING GROUPS

While the club may read the volume as a whole a different strategy would be to devote two or three sessions to the volume. The natural clusters then would be to

Session 1: Introduction and Chapters 2 to 5, Judaism, Technology and Me
Session 2: Chapters 6 to 8: Jewish Past, Jewish Civilization and Technology
Session 3: Chapters 11 to 17: Technology and the Jewish Future

## JEWISH EDUCATORS

Jewish educators in various communities of practice might utilize a different strategy

Session 1: Introduction and Chapters 2 to 5, Judaism, Technology and Me
Session 2: Chapters 9 and 10, The Four Hasidic Pockets: Eighth Graders at Heilicher Minneapolis Jewish Day School Wrestle with Technology and

Towards a Brain-Friendly and Digitally Wise Model of Learning The Heilicher 8th grade Curriculum and a Model of Brain

## RABBIS, CONGREGATIONAL LEADERS, AND JEWISH COMMUNAL WORKERS

Session 1: Introduction and Chapters 2 to 5, Judaism, Technology and Me
Session 2: Chapter 12 Jewish Conversation and Community in the Digital Age
Chapter Thirteen: Congregations in the Digital Age
Session 3: Chapters 11 to 17: Technology and the Jewish Future

## ISLAMIC AND CHRISTIAN EDUCATORS

Session One: Introduction and Chapters One to 5
Session Two: Excerpt the commentaries of Mary Hess and Terri Elton (Christian focus) or Sami Ramiz's commentaries (Islamic focus)
Session Three: Back to the Future, Chapters 14–17

# References

Adams, Henry, *The Education of Henry Adams,* 243-250 (Blacksburg:Virginia, 2012)

Agyris, Chris and Schon, Donald, *Organizational Learning II:* (Reading, Massachusetts: Addison and Weseley, 1996)

Alcalay, Reuben, *A Basic Encyclopedia of Jewish Proverbs, Quotations, and Folk Wisdom,* (New York: Hartmore House Publishers, 1973)

Alter, Adam, *Irresistible: The Rise of Addictive Technology and the Business of Keeping us Hooked,* (New York: Penquin Press, 2017)

Amkraut, Brian, "What We Know about Jewish Education in the Age of Web 2.0", in *What We Now Know about Jewish Education,* Bloomberg, Flexner, Goodman, (Los Angeles: Torah

Aura, 2008)

Angyal, Andras, *Neurosis and Treatment: A Wholistic Theory,* (New York: Penquin Press, 1973)

Aron, Isa, Sacred *Strategies: Transforming Synagogues from Functional to Visionary,* (California: Kobo Press, 2010)

Bialik, Hayim Nahman, and Ravitzsky, Yehosua Hana, *The Book of Legends,* (New York, Shocken, 1992)

Bolman, G, Lee and Deal, E, Terrance, *Reframing Organizations,* (San Francisco, Jossey-Bass, 2017)

Brookfield, Stephen, *Becoming a Critically Reflective Teacher,* (San Francisco, Jossey Bass, 2017)

Brooks, David, *The Road to Character,* (New York: Random House, 2015)

Buber, Martin, *Between Man and Man,* (New York: Routledge Classics Publishing, 2002)

Buber, Martin, *I and Thou,* (New York: Charles Scribner Press, 1970)

Buber Martin, *The Eclipse of God in the Relation between Philosophy and Religion,* chapter 7, (Princeton: Princeton University Press, 2016)

Bulka, P. Reuven, *Chapters of the Sages: A Psychological Commentary on Pirke Avoth,* (Northvale New Jersey, Aaronson Press, 1998)

Caine, Geoffrey and Caine, Renate N. Caine, *Natural Learning for a Connected World:Education, Technology, and the Human Brain,* 49-78 (New York: Teachers College Press, 2011)

Campell, A. Heidi and Garner, Stephen, *Networked Theology: Negotiating Faith in a Digital Culture,* (Grand Rapids, Michigan, Baker Academic Press, 2016)

Caplan, Eric, and Schein, Jeffrey, *The Educational Philosophies of Mordecai Kaplan and Michael Rosenak: Surprising Similarities and Illuminating Differences,* Journal of Jewish Education, Volume 80, #4, 2014

Dewar, James A., "The Information Age and the Printing Press: Looking Backward to See Ahead," 1998 Palo Alto, CA: Rand Corp., 1998)

Dewey, John, *Experience and Education,* (New York: Touchstone Press, 1997)

Dorff, Elliot, *For the Love of God and People: A Philosophy of Jewish Law* (Philadelphia: Jewish Publication Society, 2007)

D'vorkes, Joshua, *The Chafetz Chayim on the Siddur,* (Jerusalem,The Jerusalem Academy of Jewish Studies, 1974)

Dweck, S Carol, *Mindset: The New Psychology of Success,*(New York: Ballantine Press, 2008)

Elmore, Richard, *I Used to Think and Now I Think,*(Cambridge, Harvard Education Press, 2011) Fackenheim, L. Emil, *Encounters Between Judaism and Modern Philosophy,* (New York: Basic Books, 1973)

Elton, Terri and Herring, Hayim, *Leading Non-Profits in a Digital World* (New York: Rowman & Littlefied, 2016)

Freeman, John, *The Tyrrany of Email,* (New York, Scribner, 2009)

Fiore, Quentin and McCluhan Marshall, *The Medium is the Massage,* 26-64, (Corte Madero, California, Ginko Press, 2001)

Finkel, Avraham Yaakov, *The Responsa Anthology,* 167, (Northvale New Jersey, Jason Aaronson, 1990)

Friedman, Lawrence J, *Identity's Architect,* 478, (New York: Scribner, 1999)

Friedman, Maurice, *A Beleving Humanism:Gleanings,* chapter 7, (New York: Simon-Schuster, 1968)

Friedman, Thomas L Friedman, *Thank You for Being Late: An Optimist's Guide to Thriving in the Age of Accelerations,* (New York: Farrar, Straus, and Giroux, 2016)

Gee, Elisabeth, Takeuchi, M. Lori, and Wartella, Ellen, *Children and Families in the Digital Age: Learning Together in a Media Saturated Culture,* (New York: Routledge Press, 2018)

Goldsmith, Emanuel and Scult Mel, Dynamic *Judaism: The Essential Writings of Mordecai M. Kaplan,* (New York, Shocken Press, 1985)

Green, Arthur, *Seek My Face, Speak My Name: A Contemporary Jewish Theology,* (Northvale, New Jersey: Jason Aaronson Press, 1992)

Heschel, Abraham Joshua, *The Earth is the Lord's,* (Woodstock, Vermont, Jewish Lights Publishing, 1995)

Heschel, Abraham Joshua, *The Sabbath,* Prologue, (New York: Farar, Straus, and Giroux, 2005)

Houseley, John, "Paul Tillich and Christian Education", *Journal of Religious Education,* Volume 62, 1967 - Issue 4

Huizinga, Jans, *Homo Ludens: A Study of the Play Element in Culture.* (London: Routledge and Kegan, 1949)

Kaplan, M. Mordecai, *Judaism as a Civilization:* (New York, Shocken Press, 1934)

Kaplan, M. Mordecai, *The Meaning of God in Modern Jewish Religion, chapter* II the Sabbath, (Detroit: Wayne University Press, 1995)

Kaplan, M. Mordecai, *Not So Random Thoughts,* (New York: Reconstructionist Press, 1966)

Kirpatrick, David, *The Facebook Effect: The Inside Story of the Company That is Connecting the World,* 1-19, (New York: Simon and Schuster Paperbacks, 2010)

Kenaan, Hagi, *The Ethics of Visuality, Levinas and the Contemporary Gaze,* introduction, (London: I.B Tauris and Company, 2013)

Kolb, Liz, *Learning First, Technology Second: The Educator's Guide to Designing Authentic Lessons,* (USA, International Society for Study of Technology in Education, 2017)

Louv, Richard, *Last Child in the Woods: Saving Our Children from Nature Deficiency Disorder,* (Chapel Hill, Algonquin Press, 2005)

May, Rollo, *Love and Will,* 104 (New York: W.W. Norton Publishing and Company, Inc, 1969)

McGonical, Jane, *Reality is Broken: Why Games Make us Better and How They Can Change the World,* (New York: Penquin Press, 2011)

Meir, Asher, *The Jewish Ethicist: Everyday Ethics for Business and Life,* (Jerusalem, Business Ethics Center of Jerusalem, 2005)

Metzker, Isaac, *A Bintel Brief: Sixty Years Of Letters from the Lower East Side to the Jewish Daily Forward,* 158-9 (New York: Behrman House Publishes, 1971)

Mickelthwaith, John, "The Message of Thomas Friedman's New Book: It's Going to Be O.K."

New York Times, Novembe 22, 2016

Miranda, Lin-Manuel, *Gmorning Gnight: Litle Pep Talks for You and Me,* (New York, Random House, 2018)

Morinis, Alan, *Everyday Holiness,* (Boulder, Trumpeter Press, 2007)

Palmer, Parker, *The Courage to Teach,* 9-33, (San Francisco: Jossey-Bass Publishers, 1998)

Palmer, Parker, *On the Brink of Everything,* 65, (New York: Berrett-Koehler Publishers, 2018)

Progoff, Ira, *At a Journal Workshop: The Basic Text and Guide for Using the Intensive Journal Workshop,* 210-228, (New York: Dialogue House Library, 1975)

Plaskow, Judith, *Standing Again at Sinai: A Jewish Feminist Perspective,* (New York: Harper Collins, 1991)

Prensky, Marc, From *On the Horizon* MCB University Press, Vol. 9 No. 5, October 2001)

Ronson, Jon, *So You've Been Publicly Shamed,* (New York, Riverhead Books, 2015)

Rosen, Jonathan, *The Talmud and the Internet,* 10-11,(New York, Farar, Straus, and Giroux, 2000)

Schein, Jeffrey, *Technology: So Pervasive in Jewish Living, So Absent from Jewish Educational Research, (*Journal of Jewish Education, Volume 82, #4, 2016)

Schon, Donald A, *Educating the Reflective Practitioner,* (San Francisco: Jossey-Bass Publishers, 1987)

Scott, Laurence, *The Four Dimensional Human: Ways of Being Digital World,* (London, William Heineman, 2015)

Scult Mel, *Communings of the Spirit, The Journals of Mordecai M. Kaplan, Volume 1 (New York, Reconstructionist Press, 2002*

Scult, Mel, *Communings of the Spirt, The Journals of Mordecai M. Kaplan, Volume II,* (Detroit, Wayne State University Press, 2016)

Sherwin, Byron, "The Earth is the Lord's and a Passion for Turth: A Review", *Shofar: An Interdisciplinary Journal* (Purdue Press), 183-187, Volume 26, Number 1, Fall 2007

Shramm, Peninah, *Tales of Elijah the Prophet,* (New Jersey: Aaronson Press, 1997)

Smith, Larry, *Things Don't Have To Be Complicated: Illustrated Six-Word Memoirs by Students Making Sense of the World:* (New York: Simon and Schuster, Ted Books, 2012)

Solovietchik, Joseph, The *Lonely Man of Faith, chapter* 1-3, (New York: Doubleday Religion, 1992)

Steinberg, Milton, *A Partisan Guide to the Jewish Problem,* (London: Charter Books/ Bobbs Merrill, 1963)

Tapscott, Don, *Grown Up Digital: How The Net Generation Is Changing Your World,* New York: Mc Graw Hill Publishers, 2009

Turkle, Sherry, *Alone Together,* (New York, Basic Books, 2011)

Turkle, Sherry, The *Second Self: Computers and the Human Spirit,* (New York: Simon and Schuster, 1985)

Turkle, Sherry, *Reclaiming Conversation: The Power of Talk in a Digital Age,* 21-29, (New York: Penquin Press, 2015)

Wiener, Aharon, *The Prophet Elijah in the Development of Judaism: A Depth-Psychological Study,* chapter on Elijah in Hasidic Thought, (London, 1978).

Wolfson, Ron, *The Self-Renewing Congregation,* (California, Kobo Press, 2012)

# Index

# About the Commentators

**Dr. Brian Amkraut** is the director of the Laura and Alvin Siegal Institute for Life Long Learning at Case University.

**Imam Sami Aziz** is the director of spiritual life at Depauw University.

**Rabbi Michael Cohen** is the Director for Community Relations for the Friends of the Arava Institute and teaches conflict resolution at Bennington College in Vermont.

**Rabbi Elliot N. Dorff**, Ph.D., is Rector and Distinguished Service Professor of Philosophy at American Jewish University.

**Peter Eckstein** is the Director, Israel Programming and Educational Technology for the Jewish Federation of Palm Beach County.

**Dr. Terri Martinson Elton**, Associate Professor of Leadership at Luther Seminary, St. Paul, MN, teaches and consults in the areas of congregational leadership, leading change and innovation, and reimagining faith formation in the 21st century.

**Amelia Gavurin** is a 2016 graduate of Johns Hopkins University who specializes in community engagement for non-profit organizations.

**Rabbi Hayim Herring**, Ph.D., is an author, presenter, and organizational futurist specializing in "preparing today's leaders for tomorrow's organizations."

**Mary E. Hess** is Professor of Educational Leadership at Luther Seminary, where she has taught since 2000.

**Rabbi Nathan S. Kamesar** is the Associate Rabbi of Society Hill Synagogue in Philadelphia, a former attorney, and was the Managing Editor of the Berkeley Technology Law Journal.

**Rabbi Marc Margolius** is a Senior Programs Director at the Institute for Jewish Spirituality, where he specializes in integrating Jewish mindfulness practice with *middot*, spiritual/ethical qualities.

**Dr. Adina Newberg** combines teaching Hebrew language and literature with research focused on Israelis who are engaged in liberal Batey Midrash (houses of study) as a way of creating new meaning in their Jewish identity.

**Rabbi Steve Sager** is the director of *Sicha*, a Jewish project utilizing the riches of Jewish tradition to add meaning to individual and communal lives.

**Rabbi David A. Teutsch** is the Wiener Professor Emeritus and Senior Consultant to the Center for Jewish Ethics of the Reconstructionist Rabbinical College.

**Rabbi Mira Beth Wasserman**, Ph.D., is director of the Center for Jewish Ethics and assistant professor of rabbinic literature at the Reconstructionist Rabbinical College.

**Etan Weiss** is the Director of Jewish Life at the Milton Gottesman Jewish Primary Day School of the Nation's Capital.

# About the Author

**Jeffrey Schein** is a Jewish educator. He became a Reconstructionist Rabbi in 1977 and in 1980 earned his doctorate in education from Temple University. For 25 years he guided Jewish educators through the masters of Jewish education program at Siegal College in Cleveland. He presently works as the senior education consultant for the Kaplan Center for Jewish peoplehood and also directs the Text Me: Ancient Jewish Wisdom Meets Contemporary Technology project. He has authored a dozen books and several dozen articles about contemporary Jewish and religious education.  He and his wife "Dr. Deb", a trainer of early childhood educator and pioneer in the exploration of children's spirituality, moved to Minneapolis in 2015 so that they could continue their work in closer proximity to their grandchildren.